MY FATHER'S KIDNAPPING AND RETRIEVAL IN PAKISTAN

A father's nightmare and a
son's desperate struggle to save him

SYED S. SAQIB

Copyright © 2017 by Syed S. Saqib

www.syedssaqib.com

All rights reserved. No part of this publication may be reproduced, distributed, or transmitted in any form or by any means, including photocopying, recording, or other electronic or mechanical methods, without the prior written permission of the publisher, except in the case of brief quotations embodied in critical reviews and certain other noncommercial uses permitted by copyright law.

The scanning, uploading, and distribution of this book via the Internet or via any other means without the permission of the author is illegal and punishable by law.

For permissions contact:

info@syedssaqib.com

First Printing, 2017

Printed in the United States of America

Library of Congress Cataloging-in-Publication Data has been applied for.

ISBN 978-0-9993091-0-0 (Paperback)

ISBN 978-0-9993091-2-4   (eBook)

ISBN 978-0-9993091-1-7 (Hardcover)

ACKNOWLEDGEMENTS

I cannot imagine thanking anyone before God, who has blessed me with good health, a great family and a personality to deal with any difficulty in life.

I extend my special thanks to my parents who raised me and allowed me to become a good and kind human being that I am today. Without their continued guidance and support I would not be who I am today.

I remain thankful to my wife and two beautiful sons, who have been very understanding all along the way during this worst ordeal of my life time. They have been a source of inspiration and courage no matter what type challenges I faced in Pakistan rescuing my father from the ugly hands of his enemies.

Last but not least, I extend my thanks to *Hannah Sandoval*, my copy editor. She brought a lot of good insights while editing this manuscript. She did an excellent job fact checking and pointing out any uneven flow in the story. It allowed me to tweak some parts of the manuscript to make it a much smoother read for you, the reader.

CONTENTS

Preface vii
Chapter 01 - An Unhappy Reunion 1
Chapter 02 - Crossing Paths with Kidnappers 15
Chapter 03 - Kidnapped! 23
Chapter 04 - Attempted Murder on the Motorway 31
Chapter 05 - Pleas, Bargains, and Dismissals 35
Chapter 06 - Money Magic 53
Chapter 07 - The Long Journey Home 67
Chapter 08 - Watch Your Back 77
Chapter 09 - Meet Our Attorney: Mr. Iqbal 91
Chapter 10 - True Rags to Riches Story 101
Chapter 11 - Growing up in Pakistan 121
Chapter 12 - My Ride Along with Police 145
Chapter 13 - The Norwegian Narcotics Chief 149
Chapter 14 - With Friends Like These 159
Chapter 15 - Prime Suspect 167
Chapter 16 - Two Bumbling Cops and a Motorbike 177
Chapter 17 - It's Not Who You Are, It's Who You Know 187
Chapter 18 - Through the Wringer 205
Chapter 19 - What's up with This Camouflage? 219
Chapter 20 - The Trickster among Us 231
Chapter 21 - Muddled Motives 241
Chapter 22 - Invaders 249
Chapter 23 - Go Get 'em 261
Chapter 24 - Broken Justice 273

PREFACE

A violent crime befell my father because others desired what he had—the possessions and successes he had toiled his whole life to achieve. When I saw him bloodied and beaten in the aftermath, I knew I would do almost anything to make sure the culprits paid for their crimes. It soon became clear that I would have to take on the role of a detective, and I did my best to fill those shoes. If you had told me, before all of this happened, that I would ever find myself doing something like this in my life, I would have laughed. Me? A detective? Never—at least not outside of childhood games and imaginings. Perhaps you can tell me if I succeeded when you reach the end of this memoir. I'm still not sure.

My trip to Pakistan in February 2016 was meant to be a happy family reunion, but it turned into something sinister. Even now, it doesn't feel real. It's more like something pulled from a bizarre noir movie, except in those films the detective is hardened and experienced, not an asset portfolio manager. However, like a movie, the case was brought to me by a damsel in distress. I was barely in Pakistan for half an hour when my sister, Fiza, told me she had no idea where our father was, and my nightmare began.

You cannot fully understand the terror I felt in that moment unless you have ever suspected a loved one was in peril. If you've lost track of a child in the supermarket or waited for a spouse at the kitchen table long after he or she was meant to arrive home, then you've experienced that horrible drop of your gut, the pounding of blood in your ears, and the involuntary, anxious wringing of your hands.

When at last the mystery of my father's location was solved, and we learned he'd been abducted by thieves after his life's wealth, it opened a whole new mystery—one with many dark, foggy alleyways to wander down, never knowing what malignant figure might be waiting when the haze cleared. The questions never ended. Who wanted my father's wealth? What sort of people were so void of empathy that they could torture an elderly man to the brink of death?

From the moment I found my father—the man who had raised and cared for me—battered and robbed of the possessions he'd worked so tirelessly for, I was faced with a moral dilemma: remain in Pakistan to uncover the truth and help my father back on his feet or return to the US for the sake of my two young children and wife. I decided to stay as long as I could, but as things became more dangerous and my own life was threatened, the pleas from my wife to come home grew stronger.

I learned quickly to trust no one. Does it sound cliché? Sure. But when the enemy seems to know too much about you and your family, you begin to regard friends or anyone who recently came into your family's life with suspicion. You begin to analyze everything they say and do. You begin to look over your shoulder when you go out alone.

If you're American or from any Western country, you're likely wondering why I felt the need to "act the sleuth." The short answer is that the Pakistani justice system is broken. In any Third World country, resources are very limited, and law enforcement is not excluded from that. If you are not from a Third-World country, this may be hard to understand, so allow me to put it in perspective. Imagine a police station, which has jurisdiction over a major residential area, with only one cruiser. Imagine that the police officers are paid wages that only amounts to something like $100-$200 a *month*. A culture of bribery is born. Officers have little training. They don't have the resources to track criminals. They are also hampered by the court system. If you think court proceedings take forever in America, you're in for a truly nasty surprise if, God forbid, you ever find yourself dealing with a Pakistani court. If you want a legal matter resolved, you must jump through hundreds of hoops and perhaps wait years to truly "get your day in court." That is, unless you are willing to stand your ground, do most of the legwork yourself, and keep pushing authorities with relentless fervor. The reason most people never get justice in Pakistan is because the whole system is so slow, convoluted, and resource-starved that people give up before they even really get started. They have lives to live. They don't have the time or the funds to deal with the politics. But I wasn't going to let my father's case get lost in the sludge. So, to get him justice, I put on many hats: detective, negotiator, secretary, personal investigator, caregiver, and of course, son.

I was met with opposition at every turn because, though I grew up in Pakistan, after so many years in America, I had to rewire myself to think, speak, and act as Pakistani people do if I wanted anything done. In my personal opinion, Pakistan is a nation consisting of individuals who are "half emotional" and "half irrational." I would further add that these two personality traits function on a pendulum that is susceptible to wild swings between the two states. This makes

Pakistanis very complicated people to deal with in general, as I can attest to personally. In my case, this odd trait made discussions with law enforcement and court officials feel like trying to run through air as thick as soup. There is no pattern to it, only sporadic mood shifts. By the end of a conversation, you are often left scratching your head thinking, "What does he want from me?" Should you try to appeal to this person's emotions, his irrational side kicks in and confuses you, and when you try to bring some rationality into the equation, his emotional side swerves off into unknown territory and drives you crazy.

When dealing with authority figures whose minds operate this way and whose culture views bribes as a perk of the job, you are left wondering if these less-than-helpful authorities are actually constrained by the limitations of their resources or whether they are intentionally creating roadblocks to extort a bribe. Every proposition, every question, every request had to be spoken and acted upon with delicacy. If I made the wrong move, I might offend an upstanding lawman or lose an opportunity to get an important voice of authority on my side.

As I tiptoed my way through the justice system, I began to compile a list of potential suspects. The police weren't doing it, so someone had to. Many of my father's associates became suspects. Along with my sister and brother-in-law, I combed through everyone in my father's life. As a successful, self-made business man, my father had enemies. One in particular quickly went down on my list. But I knew I couldn't exclude friends, either. As the weeks went on, three names emerged above the rest, but who of them was the true villain? I tried my best to observe them from afar, find some clue, but as I worked, innocents were placed in the crosshairs of police, while the real culprits almost slipped away. My family's lives were threatened more than once. But where was the threat coming from?

Over the next four months, I searched for that answer, but at the same time I had to restore a reasonable level of order in my father's life. No easy feat. Thanks to his kidnappers and their nefariously clever scheme, we had to prove that my father truly was the owner of his own properties. Thanks to their brutal treatment, my father hardly had the strength to appear in court to battle for his own possessions. I had to take the helm and act as his cheerleader, but as a US citizen who emigrated from Pakistan back in 1998, I was regarded as a foreigner by Pakistani authorities. I tried to use this to my advantage. The Supreme Court of Pakistan has a special complaint wing for foreigners, providing them with expedited due process in courts in case they have been stranded in Pakistan due to unforeseen circumstances. I immediately requested this expedited service to help my father. But US–Pakistani relations are not what they should be, and my father was not a foreigner. I was caught in the middle, neither respected as a true local nor aided as a helpless foreigner. My dual status caused some eyebrows to raise in suspicion, and my motives were questioned. Was I a spy trying to understand the inner workings of the Pakistani government, or was I really a loving son genuinely trying to help his father out of an ordeal? In a culture of conspiracy theories, I had to move cautiously so as to not raise any red flags.

It is incredible how difficult it is just to follow due process within the Pakistani justice system. It is something Pakistani citizens struggle against on a regular basis. Criminals understand the brokenness of the system and the resource crisis that ties authorities' hands. They wear that knowledge like a badge. It gives them free rein to commit whatever sneaky, dishonest, and even violent acts they wish, because the system wears down and defeats those who actually have something to lose.

I understand that all of this sounds exaggerated or unbelievable to Western readers. I also understand that most of my readers will know little about Pakistan and its culture (apart from what they hear on American media). That is why this book will lead you along with me through not only my father's harrowing tale, but also through the streets and towns of Pakistan so that you can better comprehend this story of attempted murder, theft, deceit, struggle, and familial love.

The story began in February 2016, but it did not end until June of that year, when the true culprit's name finally came to light. Those four months felt like four years. They gnawed at my sanity and whittled down my body. You might be surprised by the face that stares back at you in the mirror when for four months, your mind has sat on the edge of a razor, fearing for your life and those of your loved ones. I often thought of my boys, just three and six. For their sakes, I often thought of putting Pakistan behind me. Didn't they have every right to grow up with their father? But getting on that plane meant leaving my father to fend for himself. Who deserved my attention the most? My father or my family in the US?

This conflict of moral obligations had no clear-cut answer. How can one choose between the boys he is meant to raise and the man who raised him? Unable to answer, I turned my focus to solving the mystery of who had placed us all at this crossroads. Well, I found the answers, but unlike a classic black-and-white film, the ending is not tied up neatly in a satisfactory moment of clarity and justice.

What is justice? Did my father receive it? If not, will he ever? I'm not certain I know the answer. Perhaps you can help me.

CHAPTER 01

AN UNHAPPY REUNION

"Bhai!" my sister Fiza called as I exited the secure area of the Islamabad airport—a name which means "elder brother" in Urdu.

She was waving at me from the crowd behind the barrier. I smiled and started to move toward her as she left the crowd and moved to meet me. She was alone. Odd. My father ought to have been with her. Perhaps he was looking for parking.

My smile slipped when Fiza got closer. We hadn't seen each other in years, and I had so been looking forward to spending a much needed vacation with her and Dad, but her expression did not give me the warm and fuzzy feeling I'd anticipated. I had expected her to be carrying her new son. Where was he? I also thought it strange for my dad to send Fiza alone.

She greeted me with big hugs and pleasantries, but it was not long before I landed on the obvious question.

"Where is dad, sis?"

"I'll tell you in a second," she said. "Let's get out of here first; it's too noisy."

Now I sensed something was wrong. She hurried out of the greeting area with me at her heels. I insisted she let me know that everything was okay. The worried look on her face and her dampening eyes did not sit well with me. We crossed the road where cars sat in lines, waiting to pick up passengers, and found a relatively quiet spot.

"Where's Dad?" I asked anxiously.

"I have no idea."

My heart dropped into my stomach.

Just that morning, February 13, 2016, had seemed like a fairly ordinary day. My wife saw me off at O'Hare International Airport in Chicago with my two sons securely tucked in their respective car seats. My elder son was six, the younger barely three. Both were there to say goodbye to their dad before his two-week-long trip to Pakistan and had already handed over their wish list of gifts. I had, deservedly, taken two weeks off from work as a portfolio manager at an asset management firm to visit my father and my sister's family in Islamabad, the capital of Pakistan. My sister Fiza and her husband Ali, both doctors at PIMS (Pakistan Institute of Medical Sciences) in Islamabad, were eager to introduce me to their nine-month-old son.

My flight started boarding at 8 p.m. and was en route from Chicago to Islamabad via Dubai, with a layover of about four hours. I landed at Islamabad International Airport around 8 a.m. local time on February 16, 2016. I went through customs and then headed to the baggage claim. There were too many people already queued around the tiny conveyer belts, which were jittering round and round, making rather squeaky noises. One end of the curved conveyer belt was so small that people were forced to stand shoulder to shoulder, looking grumpy and roughly scolding each other whenever someone made a move for a bag that turned out not to be theirs. The manners widely adopted in Western cultures are rather rare among the Pakistani general public. In developing countries such as Pakistan, India, Bangladesh, Sri-Lanka, and even China, people exhibit weak etiquette standards, and shoving and scolding is commonplace in public. Though I grew up in Pakistan, this sort of behavior is still slightly shocking and rather awkward after a long absence.

I endured it for half an hour, standing by the conveyer belt, looking for my baggage. When it puttered toward me at last, I hastily grabbed it and even said, "Excuse me," to the man who had given me nasty look earlier when I'd accidentally touched his bag. It was about 8:40 a.m. by then, and I had thought that my dad, who is always early for his appointments, and Fiza would be waiting outside—though I was not too sure about Fiza. Although she had asked me two days earlier on "WhatsApp" about the timing of my flight, I suspected she might have difficulty arriving on time with her infant son in tow.

I exited the secure area of the airport and saw a pool of people waiting to greet their loved ones behind sagging chain barriers. In this sea of people, I attempted to spot my father and hopefully Fiza, but both of them were nowhere to be seen. My father is the type who can force his way to the front, where you'll find him standing sentry, ready to wave his hand at the first glimpse of you. I walked toward the final exit, not worried in the slightest, but I kept my pace deliberately slow, expecting to hear my name shouted across the space.

I had completely exited the secured area and had reached the overly crowded common areas. Now spotting my loved ones or being spotted seemed less likely, but there was no way to head back to the secured area, as that is against airport policy. So, I slowed my pace to a near halt and it was there, not far from the main exit, that I had found Fiza at last. Her words hit me like a sledgehammer.

Dad is missing? What?

My jaw dropped.

"What?" I almost shouted.

It must have been some kind of a joke. Her expression forced me to quickly discard the thought, however.

She and our father live close together and call each other almost every other day. She even has a room set up at my father's house, and from time to time she brings a small bag of clothing and other essentials to stay there for a few days. She had actually been at his house for some time before he disappeared. So, when three days had gone by, and she had not heard from Dad, she called him, worried. She tried several times, but he never picked up. Then, about two days previously, she'd received a quick call from him. He said he was okay, but he would be out of town for a few more days.

"Then he told me to go back to my house and stay away from his place until he got back," Fiza said. "Strange, right?"

He hadn't given any explanation.

"He sounded very nervous, and like he was in a hurry," Fiza said now. She had tried to ask him for further details, but he'd just said that he would call later and hung up abruptly. Fiza tried calling his number back, with no answer. After numerous calls had gone unanswered, Fiza heard Pakistan's standard automated message tell her, "The number you have dialed is powered off . Please try again later." With no voice mail message service in Pakistan at the time, Fiza had little choice but to simply hang up and return to her home on the PIMS campus.

"Where is your son, sis?" I asked, suddenly anxious about the answer.

To my relief, she said that her girlfriend's mother was babysitting her son back at her car. We headed for the car, but Fiza had forgotten where she'd parked. While we went in circles around the parking lot, I bugged Fiza for more details, but she insisted that we find the car first so we could sit down and really talk. So, as we wandered around the lot, my bewildered mind had little to do but run hundreds of scenarios about what could have happened to my father. When we at last found the car, I greeted Fiza's girlfriend's mother, who had my nephew playing in her lap. He, at least, seemed quite jubilant.

Don't you sometimes think that kids are the luckiest people in the world?

The babysitter seemed privy to the whole situation, and my blank face while greeting her didn't appear to bother her too much.

Fiza's car was rather small, and with three adults and a car seat shoved inside, and limited space in the trunk, fitting my luggage was a challenge. However, I did manage to squeeze into the front seat. Fiza drove away from the airport in Rawalpindi toward Islamabad. We took a route that would allow us to drop off my nephew's babysitter to meet her husband in the park, and all during the forty-five minute drive, I pressed Fiza for more about Dad's whereabouts. To my dismay, there was not much more she could tell me.

In an attempt to cheer us a little, Fiza's girlfriend's mother, whom I referred to as "Aunty" (this is a common title in Pakistan for any woman of your parents' age), talked about her daughter, who happened to live in Chicago, just like me, and who was about give birth to a child. Aunty was leaving for Chicago in a week's time to help her daughter after childbirth. So, we traded numbers, and I promised aunty that if I made it back to Chicago while she was still there, I would make sure to go see her.

As we circled the massive park, trying to find the correct gate where Aunty was to meet her husband, a thought ran through my mind. I had planned to stay at my father's house, but was it secure? I was suddenly concerned about the safety of my important documents, such as my passport. My gut told me that I was better off leaving my very important belongings somewhere else. And did I really want to stay alone in the home my father had warned Fiza to stay away from. I made an impromptu decision.

"Aunty, can I ask you for a favor?"

"Sure."

"Since my father is missing, I won't be going to his house. I'll be staying with Fiza instead. Can I leave a bag of my important belongings with you? I've got a nasty feeling. If, God forbid, someone has done something to Dad, they may come for Fiza next. I think it would be best to keep all of my important things in the care of someone who isn't a family member."

"Yes, of course, dear."

So right there and then, I transferred by US Passport, American IDs, cash, and some other stuff into a bag and handed it over to Aunty before saying goodbye.

We pulled up to Fiza's home inside the four walls of the PIMS campus around 10:30 a.m. on February 16, 2016.

We sat down and waited for my brother-in-law, Ali, to return from work as a cardiologist. About an hour later, he walked through the door and announced that the PIMS police (hospitals in Pakistan have their own small police departments to assist in cases where an injury occurred as a result of a crime) had received a call from the police department of a remote city in Pakistan called Shahpur, located some 300km (about 186 miles) away. Shahpur police claimed they had detained a man by the name of Yusuf Mubashar, who claimed to be the father-in-law of Dr. Liaqat (Ali). Mr. Mubashar had requested that Dr. Liaqat get help from local police and come get him. Unless someone was posing as my father and using his name, we'd found him! Ali had immediately gotten in touch with Shahpur police. I don't exactly recall whether he was able to talk to my father or not, but as this information was from one police department to the other, there was no doubt about its authenticity.

I quickly did some online research on Shahpur and learned that it is located in the district of Sargodha about four hours away from Islamabad. I also called my wife to briefly let her know what was happening. Ali didn't even sit down after greeting me and exchanging some pleasantries. Instead, he called PIMS police once again to confirm the address of the police station in Shahpur. The officer on the other end promised to call back with directions.

There I was, freshly landed from a twenty-four hour flight from Chicago, reeling with the knowledge that my father was nowhere to be found. My hopes of a happy get-together had been crushed on arrival. I hadn't seen Ali for years, and I hadn't been able to sit down with him for even a minute. I had only just arrived at my sister's home, yet we were talking about leaving Islamabad for Shahpur, a city which was probably remote with unfriendly driving conditions. It was a real life drama playing out in front of my eyes.

Journey Toward Shahpur

Needless to say, we started packing our bags. I advised Fiza to stay home, to think of her son and how miserable he would be on a long drive, but she silenced my protests with a look. Ali did his share of asking her to stay home, but he, too, gave up shortly thereafter. Her expression of concern and determination made it hard to argue with her. How could I blame her? I felt the same.

We packed a few important items in backpacks, including the baby's formula and diapers, and headed out. It was at this point that Ali chose to reveal that he was not comfortable driving long distances. He asked me to drive. A quick, disbelieving glance to Fiza told me that he was serious. Driving in Pakistan is daunting, especially for someone used to a right-hand traffic system. Adapting to the left-hand traffic system is only the beginning, though. The roads are not well paved, and to add to the misery, there is no respect for traffic laws among the general population. Some might argue that traffic laws are somewhat followed in a major city such as Islamabad, but once you enter remote areas, it's literally like driving in a wild racing video game. The only difference is, it's real, and there are dire consequences if things go wrong. My only consolation was that, as a former resident of Pakistan, I was pretty sure my brain would soon adapt to the driving conditions. Nevertheless, being thrust into the driver seat without any warning or practice was not the best feeling.

We hit the road at about 1 p.m. local time, with me in the driver's seat. We still did not have the exact directions to the Shahpur police station. I was just following general directions toward the town, waiting on a phone call from police for exact directions. Phone GPS was not an option. My smart phone was not functional for one. Secondly, online map data is not available in developing countries, especially when you are going into rural areas.

We didn't have to wait long for the call. Ali promptly handed over the phone to me while I was trying to concentrate on driving. I almost shouted, "Seriously?" but I kept quiet and took the call. I had to park the car on the shoulder to jot down the directions.

With little time to waste, we decided to eat in the car. I took an exit ramp off the highway and spotted a small food stand, inside of which a man stood flipping burgers. Fifteen minutes later, we drove off with our fresh-to-order burgers, and they turned out to be some of the best that I have ever eaten in my life! So good that three months later I made it a point to return and get another. So at least there was one consolation.

Driving to Shahpur was half easy and half wild adventure. When you leave Islamabad city, basically your only option is to take a major highway called the "Motorway," which has been built to the modern highway standards of any First World country (actually, it is better than some of the highways I have traveled in the US). The total trip time was supposed to be four hours, with two hours on the Motorway and two hours on dirt roads outlying Shahpur. The last two hours turned into four due to the growing darkness and the dirt roads' driving conditions. Needless to say, I was feeling extremely bad for the baby. Looking back, I commend him on how well he did on the trip, and I'll be sure to relay this story to him when he grows up.

These rural roads are shared by anyone and anything you can possibly imagine, from buggies to donkeys to rickshaws, not to mention trollies hauling sugarcane from nearby fields. Then you have buses and trucks that sneak up behind you and try to pass while constantly honking their pressure horns—a common tactic to get ahead of you. The sugarcane trollies are some of the worst, though. A trolley is basically a tractor that is towing a large bed full of freshly harvested sugarcanes. The problem is that sugarcane shoots jut out from both sides of the tractor bed, blocking the whole paved area of the already small road. You have to veer off from the narrow strip of paved roadway onto the dirt shoulder to avoid being brushed by these shoots or risk breaking your windshield, for which the farmer would not take any liability. Car insurance—or farmer insurance, for that matter—is nonexistent in Pakistan, meaning you not only risk an accidentally broken windshield, but also potentially serious injuries in case of a collision that will not be covered by anyone but yourself.

To make matters worse, these trollies are hard to spot at night, as rural towns have no streetlights. When a tractor-trolley approaches you from the distance, you cannot make out whether it's a trolley, a car, a truck, a bus, or even two motorcycles side by side. If a trolley is coming toward you from the front, you risk a head-on collision with the sugarcane shoots stretching out past the bed. The farmers have learned that the best way to warn you in the dark is to switch off their headlights for a second. That way your headlights capture the full frame of the tractor-trolley, giving you a glimpse of how far the shoots are springing out onto your side of the road.

Please see a picture below of a bus accident caused by one of these sugarcane trollies. Needless to say, the bus driver was killed. This accident happened on April 10, 2016, on the same dirt roads I was driving in February.)

An accident cause by sugarcane trollies where a bus driver was killed (file photo, April 2016).

By 8:30 p.m., we were approaching Shahpur city limits. Since there were no road signs, I stopped the car at a restaurant and asked where the police station was to make sure I was on the right road. It turns out that Shahpur is divided into two areas, Shahpur City and Shahpur Sadar, and since both of these have their own police stations, we were asked which one we wanted to go to. After much aggravation, we finally concluded that it was the Shahpur City police station we needed. We finally drove up to the front gate of the station around 9 p.m.

Seeing my father and getting the shock of a lifetime

Thanks to a cumbersome practice in Pakistan called load shedding, which basically means that the power grid is turned off, causing a blackout for one hour every three hours, there was no electricity in the station when we arrived. The power company does this to "shed some load" and relieve the power grid, which could otherwise blow up due to overcapacity.

When we entered the station, we found officers going about their usual business using lamps and torchlights to find their way around. We were greeted and ushered toward an even darker side of the station where we were finally asked to enter a dark, dingy room.

The image that greeted me in that room will be burned in my memory for the rest of my life.

My father lay on a small bed, curled up against the cold. There was no mattress on the bed, only knitted strings of aged nylon that sagged almost to the floor. My healthy, seventy-year-old father now looked like a ninety-year-old man on the verge of death. It didn't seem real. It couldn't be real.

As we approached him, he tried to get up but could not find the strength to do so. The sagging nylon gave him no support. I lifted him myself, and after a slight struggle, he sat upright on the bed. Still, I did not let him go, but hugged him to me instead. Fiza sat next to him; baby cuddled to her chest, and placed her hand on his shoulder, hoping to provide some comfort with her touch.

"Dad, what happened? How did you get here? Are you sick?" I asked.

He just shook his head, his breaths shallow and labored.

"One question at a time, Bhai," said Fiza. She searched our father's face with concerned eyes.

"Dad, what happened?" I asked, trying to keep myself calm.

He tried to speak, but the words were not fluid. After only a few words, he would gulp and be forced to take a breath.

"They… they wanted the house, the properties," he murmured. "She tricked me."

"What? Who?" said Ali from his place in the doorway.

"You mean someone did this to you?" I asked, the first spark of rage igniting in my gut.

He nodded, his head drooping as he tried to stay upright.

"Who, Dad, who?" said Fiza.

"The new renter, Sadaf," my father said, lifting his eyes to mine with great effort. "We… we were going to do business with her government. She said she would drive me, but she brought me to them."

"Who?" I prompted.

He shook his head slowly. "I don't know. They wore masks. They were in the car. They… they took me somewhere." He shut his eyes tight and shook his head again.

"You were kidnapped?" I nearly shouted. Fiza, Ali, and I exchanged open-mouthed looks of shock and horror.

My father nodded his head. "Awful things," he said, voice strained and eyes closed against reality, reliving the past. "They did awful things."

It took a long time, huddled there together in that cold room, before my father was able to articulate everything that had happened. The horrendous details came slowly.

For days, he had endured his kidnappers' relentless torture. They wore blank masks that wiped their faces of any empathy or emotion each time they appeared before him. They beat him, forced a piece of cloth inside his mouth, and taped it for prolonged periods of time so he could not scream. They inserted a plastic rod in his anus when he refused to sign the checks they'd stolen from his house. Tears of pain and shame filled his eyes when he told us that, his voice soft and labored. The sight twisted my heart into a knot. They chained him up by the side of a bed and threatened to break his legs if he did not sign, waving the rod as though they were about to strike his femurs. At one point, a kidnapper had put a gun to his head while the others taunted, "Go ahead and fire." They had physically and mentally tortured an elderly man, left him beaten and broken. But who were they? My father had not recognized any of their voices, had never gotten any good looks at their faces. Why had these masked monsters committed such atrocities?

I was determined to find out.

CHAPTER 02

CROSSING PATHS WITH KIDNAPPERS

In order to unravel the mystery of my father's kidnapping, you need to understand a few things.

Description of my father's house

My father's house, where I grew up, was purchased in 1986. Islamabad is divided into various sectors. My father's house is located in Sector F-7. Each sector is assigned both a letter and a number, and each is about four square kilometers. Each sector is then divided into subsectors. For example, sector F-7 has four subsectors: F-7/1, F-7/2, F-7/3, and F-7/4. My father lives in F-7/1, but he owns property in other sectors, including a hotel plaza in F-10.

Since first moving into the F-7/1 residence, my father has made many improvements and has significantly expanded the place. The house is now divided into four portions:

1. The front portion of the house, which opens onto the main street. This is where my father currently lives.

2. The back portion of the house, which is almost a full-sized residence in and of itself with its own garage. It has four bedrooms, three baths, and a gate that opens onto the side street (see pictures below).

3. The first basement, which has been turned into an apartment with two beds and two baths complete with a living area and kitchen. I will refer to this as "Unit 1" or "smaller apartment" throughout this book.

4. The second basement, which has been turned into an apartment with three beds and two baths complete with a living area and kitchen. I will refer to this as "Unit 2" or "larger apartment" throughout this book.

Since my father lives by himself in the front portion of the house, he typically rents out all the other portions.

My father has done rather well in his business career, and he has a wide array of staff working for him. At any given moment throughout the day, you may come across these people in the house:

1. A butler (or personal assistant) named Peter.

2. A full-time chef who arrives at 8 a.m. and leaves at 5 p.m.

3. An office secretary who assists my father with his home office work during normal business hours.

4. A contractor and construction crew who work on various job sites as assigned.

Front side of my father's house in Islamabad. (Date: March 2016, Source: Author)

The back portion of my father's house, which he often rents out. (Date: March 2016, Source: Author)

My father has worked in the real estate investing and brokerage business since the 1980s (see the "True Rags to Riches Story" section for more), in addition to renting his own properties. According to my father, it was relatively easy to rent his extra space in previous years, but nowadays the business is slow, and he typically has a hard time finding good tenants. In late 2015/early 2016, he had been searching for renters for many months without luck, and he was becoming somewhat desperate.

Multiple renters, different backgrounds

Finally, someone employed at the US Consulate in Islamabad approached my father about renting his larger unit (Unit 2). This gentleman told my father that he had seen his name on the American Embassy website. This was not odd, because as a well-known landlord and a property dealer in Islamabad, it was relatively easy to find my father. The gentleman's name was Ghulam Yasir Abbas, and he was in his early fifties. He later became very good friends with my father. Abbas was also engaged in various side businesses, in addition to working for the American Embassy, and because my father is a businessman at heart, I think he enjoyed talking with him about his various business ventures. Furthermore, because I am currently settled in the US, I think my father has a soft spot for anything to do with the US. Various American companies are also trying to establish a presence in Pakistan, given its increasing population and growing middle class. For example, there have been various American cuisine restaurants/fast food chains that have opened in Islamabad recently, such as McDonald's, Hardees, KFC, and Burger King. In 2016, my father and Abbas had extensively discussed opening a Starbucks in Pakistan since it does not currently have any presence there.

The asking rent for Unit 2 was Rs. 200,000 ($2,000 US). A deal was struck with Abbas, and a lease agreement was signed. Abbas must have been making good money with his side businesses in order to afford this kind of monthly payment. It was Fiza, who often stayed at my father's house, who told me that my father had become exceptionally close friends with Abbas and that they spent a significant amount of time together. So much so that my father had made plans (unbeknownst to me) for me to sit down with Abbas during my visit in order to gain some business knowledge.

Soon after my father finalized the lease with Abbas, he found another potential tenant for his smaller unit (Unit 1). This time, it was a lady who worked at the British Consulate and was also engaged in real estate on the side. Her name was Sadaf. She, too, was in her fifties. When she first looked at the Unit 1, the asking rent of Rs. 150,000 ($1,500 US) immediately struck her as too high. She tried to negotiate it down, but my father would not budge. I think one reason for his inflexibility might have been the fact that the other unit was already rented out. Next time she came, she brought a female friend and introduced her to my father as her potential roommate, asking for my father's approval of two individuals sharing the space. No deal was reached. Next, Sadaf asked my father if, since they were not reaching a deal with this rental unit, they could perhaps work together on other real estate deals. These discussions took place over the course of many meetings, and Sadaf told my father she had great relations with foreign missions by virtue of her long-time involvement in real estate brokerage. One such mission was the British Consulate where she routinely helped British nationals, who came to Pakistan on various assignments, find and lease houses. So, she suggested that she and my father could potentially form a business partnership whereby both of them would assist foreign missions in lease arrangements and then split the commissions. She went on to mention that she was already actively working with a group of British people commissioned to Pakistan to rejuvenate *Qila Rawat* (English: Rawat Fort) near the city of Rawalpindi. It is common practice for poor governments of developing countries to ask rich nations for help funding and restoring historic monuments. Typically these rich nations gladly oblige because they consider preservation of historic monuments a worthy task.

One such example is the ancient civilization of *Mohenjo-daro*, dating back to 2500 BCE. When the ruins of this city were first discovered in Pakistan, quite a few wealthy nations offered assistance to the Pakistani government in order to discover artifacts and display them in museums in those countries. I think apart from preservation, there is some aspect of profit involved as well. Pakistan gets its name out as a responsible country, not to mention all the jobs that are provided to locals, while the other nation can please its citizens by bringing home artifacts of historic significance. In the end, it becomes a win-win situation.

Ruins of Mohenjo-daro, Pakistan. Mohenjo-daro was built circa 2,500 BCE with a population of approximately 40,000, one of the largest and most advanced cities at that time. (Source: File photo, Pakistan tourism corp.)

So you see, Sadaf's story about British nationals trying to restore Qila Rawat was not too far-fetched. Still, I must admit that my father put a lot of confidence in someone he barely knew.

My father agreed to partner with Sadaf, and after a few more phone calls, an appointment was finally setup for the afternoon of February 9, 2016. There they would meet with the delegates from Great Britain and discuss the exact type of accommodation they were looking for. Once the transaction was settled, my father would split the commission with Sadaf.

On the morning of February 9, Sadaf showed up at my father's house and offered him a ride to make things simpler. They began driving toward the City of Rawat, but Sadaf stopped her car near the outskirts, pulling up beside a waiting Toyota Vigo that she said was sent by the British Consulate to take them the rest of the way.

"Rawat Fort" near city of Rawalpindi (Source: Pakistan tourism corp.)

She hopped into the front, and my father slid into the back.

CHAPTER 03

KIDNAPPED!

Two men awaited my father inside the Toyota Vigo, not including the male driver. The car only drove a short distance before the men sitting next to him said, "You're under arrest!"

One of the men—whom my father vividly remembers as being in his middle fifties, sporting a moustache almost as thin as his hair, and wearing a white *shalwar kameez* (a traditional outfit of Pakistan)—told him in an extremely rude tone that they belonged to Inter-Services Intelligence (ISI) and that he was being taken in for interrogation. ISI is a strong arm of the Pakistan military, which is typically tasked to capture top level criminals and even implements war strategies in joint partnership with the Pakistan army.

My father, though very frightened, said nothing. Typically, ISI gets involved in very high profile cases. This agency holds an incredible amount of power and pretty much has carte blanche over the cases they handle, which are typically terrorism related. Scared to death, sitting frozen in the backseat, my father could not fathom why ISI would ever come after him, as he had done nothing wrong.

*Toyota Vigo, which was used to kidnap my father
(Source: File photo from Toyota website)*

Glasses covered in dark tape were forced over his eyes while the man in the white shalwar kameez threatened that if he showed any resistance, he would only get himself into more trouble.

"You are being brought to an interrogation cell where you will be questioned about your various illegal activities," he told my father.

Both men made it clear that it was in my father's best interest to cooperate with "authorities" and to just follow their direction if he wished to be released swiftly. Thus, my father did as he was told and kept quiet. They drove for three or four hours, and when they at last reached their destination, my father was asked to get out of the vehicle. He looked around. They had stopped in the middle of a remote area with nothing but trees all around save for a single run-down house. They lead my father to this house and shoved him inside a small room. What happened next will send chills down your spine.

My father was tortured!

I feel I must describe the severe torture my father endured over the course of the next few days, however difficult it might be for me; otherwise, the story would remain incomplete, in my opinion.

No sooner had my father been forced into this room than he was ordered to deliver up his car keys and whatever was in his pocket. It was then that my father realized he was not under any kind of arrest but had actually been kidnapped! From that point onward, my father began to resist demands. Sadly, his lack of cooperative caused his kidnappers to increase the severity and cruelty of their tactics.

My father parted with petty things such as his wallet, keys, and cash without any real trouble, but then he was brought a bundle of blank stamp papers. These are official papers issued by the Government of Pakistan and used in agreements enforceable in a court of law. They are standard copy-sized sheets of paper with a slight tan tint and the seal of the Government of Pakistan on the top. Penning an agreement of any significance without using a stamp paper in Pakistan is considered a financial suicide because agreements made on regular white sheets of paper cannot be enforced in a court of law. Stamp papers are not free and are used as a way for the government to collect taxes from citizens. The government sets an approximate price for a certain type of transaction, and you must use a stamp paper worth at least that price or higher to satisfy a legal transaction. A single stamp paper can cost as little as Rs. 5.00 ($0.05 US) or as much as Rs. 10,000 ($100 US). So, if you are buying a house, you would use a higher value stamp paper than if you were buying a vehicle, and so on and so forth.

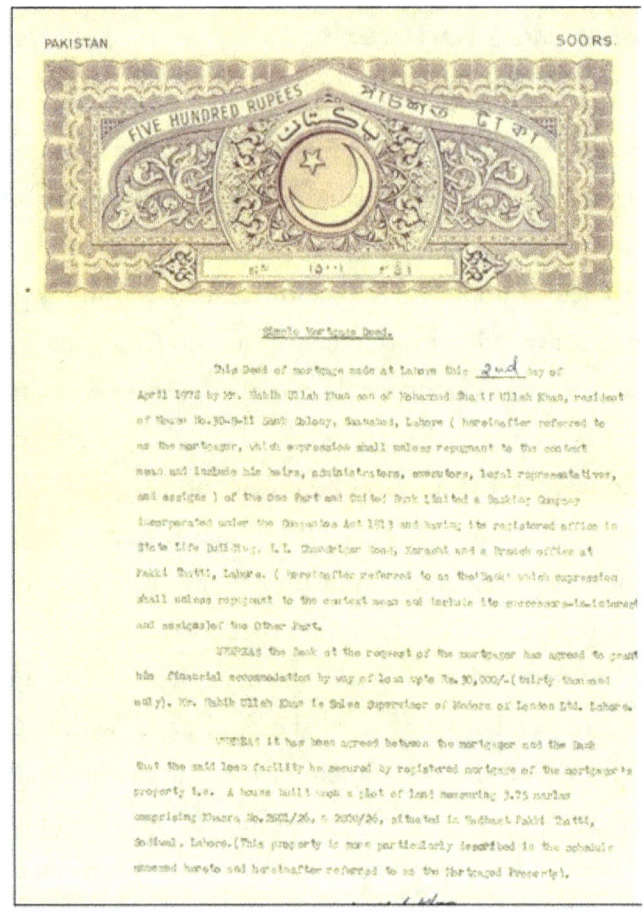

A Stamp Paper in Pakistan (Source: File photo on internet)

Because the fraud/forgery rate is quite high in Pakistan, thumb impressions are typically required in addition to signatures on legal documents. Providing a thumb impression below a signature has become a commonplace practice. So much so that sometimes courts balk at disputes involving signatures on agreements with no thumb impression.

The kidnappers presented my father with about a dozen blank stamp papers and asked him to sign at the bottom and provide his thumb impression. It was at that point that my father gave the greatest amount of resistance, outright refusing to comply.

What happened next brings tears to my eyes even now.

They inserted a long plastic rod, which they jokingly called a *mooli*, into my father's anus. (In Urdu, the official language of Pakistan, mooli means radish, also known as the daikon radish, which is long and white in appearance.)

The pure evil exhibited by these monsters toward my father is beyond comprehension. Later, when my father gave his official statement to the police (called *biyan* in Urdu), he told them that it was only after this torture tactic concluded on February 10 that he agreed to sign and give his thumb impression on all the stamp papers they presented to him.

On February 11, having confiscated my father's house keys, a few of the kidnappers (it remains unknown which) drove back to his house and burglarized it, completely ransacking the place.

I would later file a First Information Report with police listing the following items stolen:

- Deeds, registries, and title documents of all eight or nine of my father's properties

- My father's Pakistani passport(s) and his US Green Card, or Permanent Resident Card.

- My father's CNIC (Computerized National Identity Card)

- Fiza's Pakistani passport and CNIC

- My father's checkbooks for Standard Chartered Bank and Dubai Bank in Islamabad

- An unknown amount of cash
- Some valuables such as jewelry and watches
- My father's car

The most important thing stolen from the above list was the property title documents.

Why did the cook show up for work on her day off?

The odd phone calls Fiza had received from my father in the days leading up to my arrival, in which he had sounded extremely nervous and told her to stay away from his house, were actually made at gun point during these few days of torture.

While we were discussing all of these horrible events together later, Fiza recalled a phone call from my father's cook, Nina, on the morning of February 11, the day of the burglary. Nina had apparently arrived for work to find all the doors locked and no one around. Concerned, she called Fiza. Fiza told her that our father was out of town and that she could just take the day off, but after hanging up, Fiza realized it was Thursday. Thursdays were supposed to be the Nina's day off? Why had she shown up at all? Fiza and I would soon begin to wonder if she was somehow involved in the kidnapping. But how to know for sure?

Draining my father's bank accounts

After the burglary, the criminals returned to the run-down home with their loot in my father's car and asked him to sign his personal checks. My father resisted as best he could but quickly succumbed to more torture tactics, including beatings.

On February 12, 2016, Sadaf, the would-be renter, drove to Islamabad to cash the signed checks at both of my father's banks: Standard Chartered Bank in Super Market Islamabad and Dubai Bank in F-10 Markaz (Center) Islamabad. This turned out to be her undoing. Once my father was retrieved, I went to both of these bank branches with Islamabad Police and actually retrieved her ID, which put police on her trail.

Still, she had managed to withdraw about Rs. 2,000,000 ($20,000 US) for her trouble.

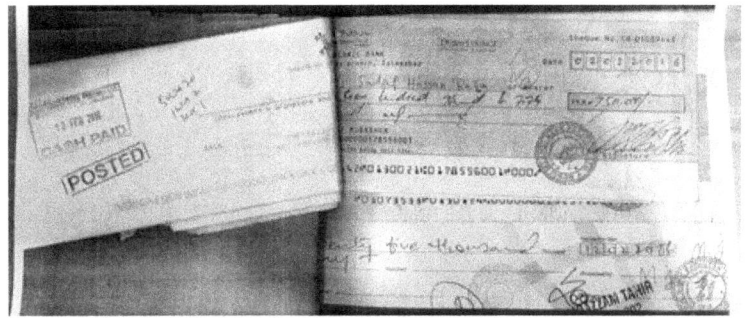

Actual photo of a check that was used to withdraw funds from my father's account at Dubai Bank in Islamabad. You can clearly see that it was drawn in Sadaf's name and that the cash was paid on February 12, 2016. (Date: March 2016, Source: Author)

CHAPTER 04

ATTEMPTED MURDER ON THE MOTORWAY

When Sadaf drained my father's accounts on February 11, a manager at one of the banks called his cell phone to inquire if the request was legitimate. My father confirmed the request at gun point.

The torture continued over the next three days. My father's legs were chained to the bedside so that he could not move, a piece of plastic was shoved into his mouth so that he could not scream, and then the plastic rod was again forced inside his anus. In addition to threatening to break his legs, one of the men would then stand over him with a gun while his partner screamed, "Shoot him!" again and again. My father later told me that at one point he actually told them to go ahead. He had little doubt that his last moments had arrived, so as he lay strapped to that bed, he prayed to God for a quick and painless death, should it come.

My father's memory of his last couple days in captivity was vague. He received no proper meal during all that time, given nothing but bits of fruits. He became extremely weak and drifted in and out of consciousness during the last twenty-four hours, close to death.

Worse still, on the last day, the kidnappers injected him with some kind of drug that made him extremely dizzy and bloated his stomach. This slow attempted murder was part of their escape plan. On the morning of February 15, 2016, once my father was heavily dosed, the kidnappers put him in his own car, taken in the burglary, and simply told him to drive—he was free. When my father asked where he was, they told him he was near City of Mirpur near Kashmir, which was not true at all. He was actually right outside Shahpur. Why the kidnappers told him otherwise remains a mystery, but the end goal was clear; my father was in no state to operate a vehicle.

He recalls very little of the drive, save being dizzy and feeling very sick. He drove on the same road Fiza, Ali, and I had taken on our way to Shahpur—the road rife with the dangers of sugarcane trolleys and oil tankers. Had my father been so unfortunate as to collide with someone on this busy highway, it would merely look like a road accident to a casual observer.

Driving away from the kidnappers

As soon as my father started driving, his car wavered all over the road. Actually this would turn out to be a blessing in disguise because, after going only a short distance, he was stopped at a police check post due to his erratic driving.

Police asked my father where he was going, to which he explained that he was leaving Mirpur and going to Islamabad. Neither was he in Mirpur at present nor was he headed toward Islamabad. Police officers immediately became suspicious and told him that he was some 350km (220 miles) away from Mirpur and that the road he was on did not lead to Islamabad. Police also noticed something unusual in the way my father was talking and behaving, so they immediately placed him under arrest.

A hideous plot by the criminals

Had my father died in a crash, as his captors no doubt had intended, they could have easily placed a claim on all of his property thanks to the signed and fingerprinted stamp papers. All they would need to say was, "Mr. Mubashar sold it to us just before his tragic demise." Presenting the stamp papers and the stolen property titles would have sealed the deal. With all of the paperwork they had in order, even the claims from me and my siblings could not have prevented the kidnappers from obtaining a deed of sale and claiming all property rights. With no evidence of foul play in my father's death, the validity of his signature and thumbprint would never be questioned.

What a hideous plot by these criminals!

There in that cold, dingy Shahpur holding room, I asked my father if he had any idea who might have done this to him.

He shook his head is dismay and said, "I'm not sure. Maybe Khan. But he wasn't there. I would have recognized his voice."

Riaz Khan was a snake of an ex-employee and business partner of my father's. They were currently locked in an ugly legal battle over a hotel property.

It's all still surreal to me. Whenever sadness grips me as I think back on my father's ordeal, I cling to the fact that it could have been worse. What if my father had died on that treacherous road? We could have done very little to regain our estate from these criminals.

My father's legacy would have been lost. Even if my siblings and I had suspected the accident was not a natural death, how could we have proved it in court? Even with a shred of proof, the system in Pakistan is so rigged and corruption is so rampant that we would have doubtless been entangled in useless litigation for years without any fruitful outcome. With my children waiting for me back in the US, I could not have fought that losing battle long. I would have burned out and returned home thinking my father's estate was never meant for me. Honestly, the hair at the back of my neck stands up just thinking about it.

Happily, that was not God's will. All my father's hard-earned assets belong to him while he is alive, and later his estate will pass to his children. This is God's will!

What wrong had my father done to provoke these criminals? Absolutely nothing. He was just an innocent victim caught up in their greed—greed so great they were willing to deprive an innocent man and his family of their estate and to inflict all manner of pain to get it. They had even attempted murder.

Are there any limits to the evil of humanity? I guess not.

CHAPTER 05

PLEAS, BARGAINS, AND DISMISSALS

My father was taken into custody on February 15. I arrived in Islamabad and made the swift journey to Shahpur on February 16 to find him nearly transformed into a skeleton.

In the interim, my father had needed immediate medical attention to prevent his death. Therefore, the whole of February 15 was spent giving him medical care so that he would be able to recall the prior days' series of events. By evening, he had recovered enough to remember a few things and to provide some information to police. It was then that he asked police to contact Fiza and Ali at PIMS. According to Ali, this call was made just as my plane was landing at Islamabad airport.

Had you known my father before any of these atrocities were inflicted upon him, the feeble, helpless state in which we found him would have been all the more appalling. I will discuss my father's incredible rags to riches story in later chapters, but for now, please take a look at the following pictures in order to get a glimpse of how he carried himself as an accomplished business man.

My father with the US Ambassador to Pakistan Wendy J. Chamberlin in Islamabad. (Date: December 2001, Source: Author)

My father (pictured in the middle) with the US Ambassador to Pakistan Anne W. Patterson in Islamabad. (Date: April 2008, Source: Author)

*My father in Times Square, New York, USA.
(Date: October 2004, Source: Author)*

My father in Shahpur police station the morning after I first found him. (Date: February 17, 2016, Source: Author)

My father in Shahpur police station. (Date: February 17, 2016, Source: Author)

After we had met briefly with our father, we immediately went to meet with the Station House Officer (SHO), who is the equivalent of a sheriff in the US. Not knowing our father, the SHO had naturally been under the impression he was a drug addict. I told him who I was and that I had landed in Pakistan that morning, travelling from the US where I have a very successful career. Ali introduced himself as a well-respected Cardiologist at PIMS hospital. Fiza also introduced herself as a doctor at PIMS. I am sure after this introduction the SHO saw my father and our family in a different light. We certainly felt his demeanor change. He eased up on us quite a bit and began to exhibit an attitude of cooperation instead of apprehension.

Although the SHO's attitude had become more cooperative, he told us in no uncertain terms that Mr. Mubashar (my father) had been arrested while driving intoxicated; therefore, police could not release him merely on our word. He further explained that police had to carry out their formal investigation. A case would be registered against him, and a suit would be filed. The only thing my father could do was claim his innocence in court. The SHO also assured us that police would conduct a thorough investigation to find out if my father was really an innocent victim of kidnapping. While I understood where the SHO was coming from, it hugely concerned me because it meant serious trouble brewing ahead. For starters, criminal cases in Pakistan can drag on for years without any good reason. We would also have to fight these charges in a town that was completely foreign to us and where we knew no one. So, when the SHO mentioned local litigation, I felt as if someone removed the ground from under my feet. Ali became nervous, too. We were determined to make sure that if there was going to be any litigation, it would commence in Islamabad and nowhere else.

Trying to get out of Shahpur

Ali performed a medical exam on my father and immediately declared it an extreme medical emergency. My father's belly was swollen to the point that he was having difficulty breathing. His body was not digesting anything, so he was not getting any energy from what he was eating and was suffering from loose stool. Most worrisome was that the substance injected by the kidnappers was building inside his body like a poison, and it might have already become deadly.

"We need to get him to a hospital for immediate medical attention and a full cleaning of his internal organs," Ali told the police. "Otherwise, he will most likely die from the poison."

Ali and I hoped my father's medical condition would act as leverage to convince police to let us go. However, the SHO insisted that that was impossible. At that point, they had no way of determining whether my father had been drugged by someone else or if he had drugged himself. My father would have to be taken to a hospital in Shahpur later on.

There were two major issues with this. First, we were not familiar with the surroundings, and this was a tiny town in a poor country where access to advanced medicine was very limited. Second, according to Pakistani law, all court proceedings must take place in the same city where the case is registered. There was no telling how long this case would drag on, and hauling my father back and forth for future court dates while he was sick would be incredibly inconvenient. Throw in the possibly corrupt system in a small city of Pakistan, and you are talking about real trouble ahead.

At that point (and perhaps mistakenly), Ali adopted an argumentative tone with the SHO, telling him that my father was in precarious medical condition and that police should put on a better show of cooperation.

"This man is an innocent victim who deserves compassion, not further punishment," he said, voice raised.

Ali's harsh tones made me nervous. Arguing with police wouldn't get us anywhere, especially since, in all fairness, they had a point.

Asking police to just let a possible criminal, caught "red-handed" with drugs in his system, walk out of the station was pushing it. Though it must be said that sometimes, in Pakistan, police can release anyone at their whim and never be questioned, police had no proof of innocence and arguing with them would do more harm than good.

So, I chimed in, cutting off Ali as fast as I could, and brought the focus back to our father's medical condition. I warned the SHO that if my father was not treated immediately, he might die right there at the police station. The SHO was suddenly very attentive. I tried my best to convince him that my father should be seen by his family doctor in Islamabad first, but he didn't totally bite. He told us to take my father to a local hospital as soon as possible.

While this was something of a relief, there was still one major problem.

"If we keep him in Shahpur, will you register the case locally?" I asked.

He nodded.

I explained to him that that would cause unnecessary hassle for my father (and us) down the road. I told him my father was kidnapped from Islamabad, so a police case would need to be registered there, too. I told him that, given the circumstances, it just made sense for my father to receive all medical treatment in Islamabad where he already had a trusted doctor.

It was the last trick in my bag, but the SHO would not budge. I think that my father's case had already become high profile, at least by local standards, so the SHO feared taking responsibility for releasing him without proper procedures. Plus, there was no central database in Pakistan where he could check my father's prior police record.

However, my father's medical condition and our adamant persistence seemed to strike a chord of compassion with him. He made us a deal.

Call to the DCP and his shocking response

He offered to call his boss, the Deputy Commissioner of Police (DCP) and let him decide the next step. The SHO promised us that if the DCP agreed to let my father go, we could take him home right then and there. I thought it was a fair offer, but I also knew he was going to make the call anyway to seek his senior's opinion. However, what he said next convinced me he was making a sincere effort. He offered to initiate the call in front of us so that we could witness the conversation. It was about 11 p.m. at night, though, and I wasn't sure how his boss would react to a late wakeup call.

So, we all gathered together in the station—my father, the SHO, Fiza, Ali, my nephew, myself, and the SHO's junior officer, the inspector—and listened.

"Sir, we have arrested an individual who was driving erratically on the highway and was severely intoxicated…"

My heart sank. However, there was nothing I could do except listen to the SHO rattle on about the incident. Finally, he mentioned that all the family members had already arrived in Shahpur. From our end, it sounded like the DCP was more interested in details of the incident rather than us. At long last, he got to the point.

"And, sir, the family members are requesting we release their father into their custody."

It was obvious, by the look on the SHO's face, that his boss had just said something along the lines of, "Are you out of your mind?"

The SHO hung up shortly after and told us it was out of his hands. The DCP had asked the SHO to present Mr. Mubashar to him at his office the next morning at around 9:30.

"This would never have happened if you hadn't made that call and had just let my father-in-law go!" Ali said, shocking us all.

I froze.

"I tried to help you the best I could, and in return all I get is this crap?" the SHO shouted back, and he stormed out of his office.

We watched him hop into his patrol car and drive off, leaving us standing with the inspector, who apprised us calmly.

"You really messed up there," he told Ali. "If you were in his shoes, you'd be mad, too."

I held my silence, not knowing what to do next. We would have to stay in town that night, but there was no way I could allow myself to sleep in a comfortable hotel bed while my father languished on his pitiful cot in the police station. Since we had already pissed off the highest-ranking officer in the police station, I had to play my cards carefully. I pulled the inspector aside for a private conversation.

"Look, what my brother-in-law said was really insensitive. You guys have been great toward my dad thus far, under the circumstances. But you have to understand that we cannot leave our ailing father here while we go sleep in a comfortable hotel room. Please let us take him along so that he can sleep comfortably as well."

His mouth gaped a little. "So, first you guys piss off my boss, and now you want to take your father off the premises? What if you never return? We would certainly lose our jobs."

Obviously his concern was legitimate, but there was still hope. The SHO was just out on routine patrol and was expected back soon.

The inspector said that when he returned, we could ask him. So we waited.

When he returned an hour later and had settled into his office, I gathered all the courage I had and went in to see him, along with the inspector.

"Sir, I really appreciate that you have given my dad more than fair treatment while he has been in your care, and I'm truly grateful for all the medical assistance provided thus far. I also appreciate your kind effort to make the call to the DCP in front us, which shows your sincerity and fairness. I think my brother-in-law's comment was hurtful to you, and I apologize on his behalf."

The SHO relaxed in his chair somewhat and then segued into a long dissertation about all that had been done for my father, emphasizing that they had allowed him to sleep on a bed instead of a cold jail cell floor.

I let him vent, and then, when he was through, dropped the bomb. "Again, thank you. However, I would like to take my father to a hotel with us."

To my amazement and disbelief, he leaned back in his chair and said, "Sure! Why not? He would be much more comfortable there with family around to take care of him."

I thanked him profusely for his kindness, overwhelmed with happiness and gratitude, and started making arrangements for the hotel.

Overnight stay in Shahpur hotel

The SHO's two conditions for my father's release were that a squad car had to follow us to the hotel and a police constable would be assigned outside the hotel all night. We had no problem with that.

When I told my father he would stay with us, he was ecstatic. We didn't waste any time gathering our belongings and leaving the station. In such a small town, the best hotel we could find was rather lackluster, but it would do. We made a quick stop at the pharmacy to pick up medicine before at last arriving at the hotel at 11:30 p.m. on February 16, 2016.

The hotel was located on the riverside and was seemingly the best option in town. It wasn't exactly a silent retreat, however. Just outside, a bridge went over the river. Traffic slowed, and truck engines hissed to a halt, loud music blaring from their cabins. On occasion, trucks honked to each other on the highway, which is actually very common in Pakistan and even considered a good thing because it warns the other party of an approaching vehicle on the narrow roads.

After a quick dinner, my father took some medication and was ready to go to sleep. We had booked two rooms. I shared one with my father, and my sister's family took the other. However, it was a restless night with all the highway noise easily slipping through the windows and thin walls of the hotel. On top of the noise, my father had to use the bathroom again and again, and he needed my assistance. Add in the anxiety about the next morning's meeting with the DCP, and it's safe to say, I did not feel rested at all when I got up around 7 a.m.

The whole family reconvened over breakfast and discussed the upcoming day. We were ready to leave by 8:30 a.m., and after a call to the SHO, requesting our escort, I started chatting with the inspector. He was the most reasonable guy in the police station, by far. He gave me some insights into the personality of the DCP and briefed me on how my father should present himself so as to increase his chances of release. He said that my father should be upfront and tell the complete truth. He also mentioned that my father should keep his tale short and to the point. He advised that my father's tone should be that of a victim subjected to heinous torture and inhumane behavior, and thus in dire need of immediate medical treatment. However, he warned that my father should purposely refrain from going into the nitty-gritty details of the torture and any other aspects of his captivity; minor confusion on the DCP's part would only mean rejection. He said, "Get to the point and keep it short and simple." He told us to emphasize that my father was a respectable citizen and had no prior criminal history.

When I look back on this conversation, I cannot help but praise this inspector's ingenuity and sincerity toward my father and me. I was quite amazed at this sound advice. Not only was he very forthcoming, but also he was acting as if he was on our side. I believe that these policemen deal with so many bad people on a daily basis that they can intuitively tell from right and wrong. I also believe that this inspector was convinced that my father was innocent, and he was sincerely trying to help.

A police vehicle finally arrived around nine, and we followed the cruiser to the DCP's office.

Meeting with the DCP

Once we were outside the DCP's office, sitting in the car, the waiting game started. Police refused to allow us to sit inside the DCP's warm and cozy sitting area since my father was still technically under arrest.

One officer made it a point to say, "Buddy, be thankful your father is not in handcuffs right now!"

My father continuously had to leave the car to go to the bathroom constructed adjacent to the main building. The only good thing about this was that the whole police force outside the DCP's office witnessed my father's misery firsthand. After a while, I asked the SHO to give the DCP a call and see where he was. He gave me a "You must not be serious?" look.

The DCP did not deign to arrive until around 11 a.m., his entourage of officers following in a police caravan. He had finished his morning rounds in the city and had at last decided to show up with all the flair and pomp of a powerful leader. When his vehicle pulled up, a constable stepped forward and opened his door for him. It's true that the DCP is quite a powerful person, especially in a small town like Shahpur. In big metropolitans, it might be a different story, but there, a DCP might be looked upon as a local god. Local businessmen pay special tributes to him, and he receives special attention wherever he goes in town. So much so, in some smaller parts of the country, restaurants even refuse to charge DCPs for meals. One main reason for the special respect is that these officials wield powers such as the ability to levy fines, cancel a license, etc., so it's in small businesses' interests to keep them happy and appeal to their egos.

The DCP paid little attention to everyone standing around him and went straight to his office without any sort of acknowledgment of us or our wait. The DCP was a tall but stout man in his late forties, evidenced by the shades of grey in his inky hair. His thick moustache covered a drawn, frowning mouth. I must say, his personality exuded a lot of authority with an aura of arrogance. I looked toward the SHO with an expression of hope. With a shake of his head, he motioned for us to stay put while he went inside to seek permission for us to enter.

When we were finally ushered inside, the DCP was sitting on a tall chair in one corner of the room facing us from across a table. Chairs lined the back corner of the room and the side walls, but my father, Ali, and I sat down in those directly across the table from him. Fiza took one in the back, holding her son in her lap. Both the SHO and his inspector sat beside the DCP. I knew we should tread with caution, as I did not know at the time if the DCP was privy to the fact that my father had stayed in a hotel with his family and not in a jail cell. I didn't want my father accused of accepting special favors and didn't want to get the officers in trouble either.

Before anyone could say a word, the DCP started ringing a bell for his peon, looking impatient. After two or three bells, the peon still did not show.

"Where the hell is he?" the DCP demanded of the SHO, though there was no reason he should know the answer.

The SHO got up from his seat and went outside to look for the worker. When the poor peon finally arrived, he received a sharp rebuke while we all sat watching, awkward and silent, in our chairs. When the chastisement ended and the worker was turned away, the DCP took out a cigarette and fumbled in his pockets for a lighter. The SHO promptly produced his own and helped the DCP light up.

I sensed Ali tense. It appeared the DCP did not realize, and probably did not care, that he was sitting across from a severely ill person. We could do nothing to stop him either. My nephew, perhaps irritated by the smoke filling the room, fussed in Fiza's lap. The DCP fixed Fiza and her child with an ugly look I did not like. In fact, I didn't like anything about the office's environment. Something foul hung in the air, and it wasn't just the smoke.

My father anxiously awaited the green light to tell his story. Unfortunately, the tense moments of waiting caused him to forget the inspector's instructions, and when the DCP finally gave the go-ahead, he launched into a winded and detailed explanation of how a woman by the name of Sadaf (unfortunately, he said he did not know her last name) had approached him as a potential renter, then asked to enter a business partnership with him, and finally tricked him into getting into a kidnapper's car.

I studied the DCP as he took impatient puffs of his cigarette and let his eyes wander the office, and my heart sank. As the story became more involved, he started to interrupt, asking things like, "So…?", "What?", and "Okay… What happened next?" It was clear that multiple points in the narrative confused him.

Suddenly, in the middle of it all, a well-dressed man wearing heavy cologne waltzed into the room without so much as a knock. He sauntered past us all and extended his arm toward the DCP for a handshake. I gawked at him, dumbfounded by his utter lack of etiquette.

His odorous cologne melded with the smoke, and my nephew whined and squirmed even more. Even I felt nauseous from the smell. It turned out that he was a local businessman and wanted to discuss some issues with the DCP. Though they seemed to know each other well, the DCP didn't appreciate his intrusion, either, and dismissed the gentleman.

After a laborious tug on his cigarette to try and coax out the few remaining puffs, the DCP asked my father to carry on. As he continued, he repeated over and over that the whole blame of his kidnapping rested on Sadaf. Hers was the only name he had in his arsenal, and he relied heavily on it, but I fear it was a mistake.

You see, Pakistan is a conservative country where women rarely commit crimes. Women are perceived as mostly innocent creatures; it is men who are synonymous with dangerous crimes, especially something as deplorable as the torture of an elderly man. Yet, my father described a woman as some kind of ring leader of a kidnapping gang. It was obvious this made the DCP uneasy. He butted in, asking the SHO, "Does this make sense to you?"

The SHO returned a weak smile, and I knew we were fighting an uphill battle. Ali sensed it, too, because he tried to chime in, but he made the mistake of starting out his introduction with the fact that he knew the Inspector General of police in Islamabad, who is far higher in rank than a DCP. Ali was merely trying to create an "in" and establish credibility, but the comment rubbed the officer the wrong way.

"Cut out the who-you-know part and get to the point!"

I tried to repair the damage, saying that we were respectable people, my father included, and that thanks to his kidnap and torture by a group of brutal criminals, we needed to get him immediate medical attention. I told him I had landed in Pakistan from United States just a day earlier – where I had a successful career as an asset manager – just to find myself in perhaps the worst dilemma of my life. We were hardworking, successful, innocent citizens trapped in a most unfortunate situation.

It was at that moment, when the DCP's face softened a fraction of an inch, that my nephew started crying.

"Could you take that child outside?" he said gruffly.

Fiza, looking offended, gathered up her baby and left.

The DCP pondered his dying cigarette. Fiza came back in while we sat in tense silence, her child cooing and calm in her arms. With one final puff, the DCP looked at his subordinates and said, "His story makes no sense to me. The woman came to get him, and he was naïve enough to ride in a car with a stranger, who then took him to another vehicle, which he again entered? And this woman and her cohorts kidnapped him from there and not at his home when she first came to get him?"

The SHO only looked at him blankly, waiting for further orders. Fiza and I exchanged a frightened, confused look.

The DCP looked at his ashtray again, where his cigarette butt smoldered. "Keep him in custody," he told the SHO before looking to Ali and I. "Go back to Islamabad and file a First Information Report at the station there. This kidnapping nonsense is in their jurisdiction. Bring that FIR and an inspector level officer back with you, and I'll release your father into that officer's custody."

We looked at each other, beaten, knowing there was no point in talking further.

"Now, please," said the DCP, waving his hand in a shooing motion, "all of you can leave."

CHAPTER 06

MONEY MAGIC

The drive back to the Shahpur police station was a melancholy one. I felt beaten, at the total mercy of the circumstances. Anger hadn't quite settled in yet; it was staved off by the shock. My head hung, my shoulders drooped. I couldn't seem to hold them high anymore. Exhaustion, disbelieve, and confusion weighed me down. When we arrived back at the police station, we passed all my father's medication and his intake schedule to the officers.

"Not the best performance," said the inspector, not unkindly. "But at least your father won't be prosecuted in Shahpur."

I had to agree, though I certainly wasn't jumping for joy over the outcome.

Naturally, my father was extremely unhappy since he was not going back home. I came up with few words of encouragement;

"Though they won't let us take you home just yet, Dad," I said, kneeling on the floor beside his bed. "But I promise I'm coming back soon. As soon as I reach Islamabad, I will head straight to the Kohsar station and file this FIR and bring back an inspector so that we can take you back with us. We'll be back tonight if I have anything to do with it."

I took his hand, and he squeezed it as best he could. "Thank you, son," he said.

"Of course," I said. "I have to go; the faster we can get there, the better."

He nodded.

"Goodbye, Dad. I love you. I'll be back," I said, holding in the tears as I hugged him again.

He told me he loved me, too, and I turned to go, hating the dark, cold, unfeeling walls that would hold him until I could return. I looked back when I reached the door, and my heart ached to see him lying in that pitiful, filthy bed, but there was nothing I could do to change it.

The inspector was waiting just outside the door.

"Please, take care of him," I said.

"I will," he said, face solemn.

"He needs to eat. Please, bring him whatever he wants. He also needs someone to make sure he's taking medication on a regular schedule. He's not doing well."

"I promise I'll look after him."

"Thank you."

Just before we left, the SHO reiterated, in a not-so-friendly tone, that we must return with an original FIR and an inspector level officer from the Kohsar police station, which had jurisdiction over my father's residence. This, at least, was good news. Ali had some contacts there, which we certainly planned to utilize.

Driving back to Islamabad

I took the wheel once again. On the journey back to Islamabad, my father called Ali on this cell and asked him to call his new tenant, Abbas, who had just rented the larger basement apartment. My father had told me that he considered the man a personal friend after I had witnessed him, with tears on his cheeks, telling Abbas over the phone all about his kidnapping story back in Shahpur.

Now my father told Ali that Abbas had promised to assist us with all police matters in Islamabad. My curiosity was peaked. I asked Fiza how long our father had known this man he was suddenly so close to, and she said about three or four months. Knowing how reserved my father is, I thought Abbas must have been a really great guy to become our father's close friend in such a short period of time.

Ali made the call to Abbas right away and gave the other man a basic rundown of what had transpired and what needed to be done next, before handing over the phone to me. Abbas sounded like a nice enough guy, but when I asked if he could provide any assistance in obtaining the FIR, his rather weak response of, "I will see what I could do for you," puzzled me. Given how highly my father regarded him, I admit I had expected more enthusiasm. I tried to give him a concrete task to make things easier. There is an application that needs to be filled out before filing an FIR, so I asked him if he could help me with that part of the process. Also I told him that if he really wanted to help, he should meet with us that night at the police station.

"Okay, I will see."

"All right, well," I said, my brow wrinkling, "we could really use your help filling out the forms."

"Oh, well, I've never done that before. I'm not sure how much help I could be." I hung up disappointed.

When we reached Islamabad after about 5-6 hours, I dropped off Fiza and her son at her house and then headed straight to Kohsar police station with Ali.

Islamabad Police and their surprises

Pakistani police operate differently than those in Western countries. First of all, this resource starved agency pick and choose what to prioritize on a whim; the rules are not hard and fast. Typically, they expect bribes if you want them to speed things up. Second, kidnappings and other heinous crimes have become rather rampant in Pakistan, and a kidnapping case does not garner as much attention as you might think. In a nutshell, there are "tricks of the trade" when dealing with Pakistan police.

When we arrived at the police station around 8 p.m. on Feb 17, 2016, we received a pretty cold response. They paid the case and us little attention. In any case, I tried to convince them that we needed two things done right away:

1. Register an FIR

2. Have an inspector-level officer accompany us back to Shahpur

The problem was that an FIR alone can take several days to be registered, even though it really only takes a short while to fill out and file. Police usually require some kind of evidence before registration, though. Plus the possibility of a bribe is always hovering in the air. I thought my father's situation was pretty straight forward, but police might think otherwise. You just never know. In our case, though, police did not flatly refuse to register an FIR, but they delayed it for reasons unbeknownst to me. First they said they were short of staff to write a report (FIRs are still handwritten in Pakistan via pen and paper). Then they said they would not have an inspector-level official available to accompany us that night anyway. They also wanted to get in touch with Shahpur police before going any further. I tried to make them understand that my father was in precarious medical condition and needed to be brought back to Islamabad as soon as possible, but all my pleas fell on deaf ears.

After it became clear we were getting nowhere, Ali brought up the name of a friend who was a cell phone dealer in the nearby Jinnah supermarket. This friend had a contract with the Kohsar police force to service their mobile phones, and he knew many officers there personally. His shop was within walking distance, so Ali and I decided to seek his help. It's odd to think that a cell phone vendor could potentially assist with police matters, but if you want to get a job done in Pakistan, it's all about knowing the right people.

The cell phone vendor turned out to be an amazingly nice guy who expressed a lot of empathy toward my father and offered all the help he could. He actually took off work and started making phone calls to his various acquaintances at the station. We listened in on his conversations with various officers as he assured them that we were trustworthy people and that our case was genuine (I don't know who makes up fake stories about their father's kidnapping, but that's beside the point). He spoke genially, but there was an underlying urgency and business-like seriousness in his voice. He requested that police cooperate with us immediately due to the health condition of my father. After getting assurances from various senior officers, he hung up and told us we would receive full cooperation when we went back. Before we did, the vendor invited us to eat at a neighboring restaurant called Captain Cook. To my amazement, he even picked up the tab. I thought that was really generous of him since he was the one who deserved to be treated for helping us. I must say that I was far more impressed by this near stranger's generosity than I was by Abbas' noncommittal assurances.

After finishing dinner, I was so exhausted I struggled to keep my eyes open, having only had a few hours' sleep since arriving at the airport, but there was still work to do. When we walked back into the station, the police announced they were ready to draft an FIR. The vendor's magic had worked. An officer started working on a draft right away. It took longer than expected because when the officer was almost halfway done, Ali and I remembered that, in our exhaustion, we had forgotten to tell the officer we suspected the kidnappers had burglarized my father's home. I also realized I'd provided the wrong date for the day Sadaf had lured my father from his home. Lastly, I thought it might be a good idea just to put Khan's name out there as a possible suspect so that police could begin looking into him, even though we had no proof. Unfortunately, this meant the officer had to scrap his former sheets of paper and start all over again. This was a huge waste of time, but I was the claimant on my father's behalf and would be someone responsible for the truthfulness of its contents, so I wanted it done right.

February 17th slipped into the 18th before the FIR was completed. Then we hit another snag. The SHO there, Malik Bashir, said that he could send a constable with us back to Shahpur, but there was no inspector available that late at night. Tomorrow morning would be worse, as a political rally was scheduled and the whole force would be deployed there. I told him that bringing anyone other than an inspector risked us getting turned away by the Shahpur SHO.

Officer Bashir appraised me with compassion in his eyes and picked up his phone. He called his counterpart in Shahpur and talked to him about accepting a junior level official. When he hung up, he told me that Shahpur police had agreed to release my father into the custody of a constable. I was really thankful to Kohsar police station SHO for doing this favor for me. I was and still remain truly thankful to Officer Bashir for his help that night and in later months.[1]

Driving back to Shahpur, once again!

It was already 2am by the time a constable was found. I tried my best to mentally prepare myself for another harrowing four to five hour drive in total darkness. On a hunch, I stopped by Fiza and Ali's house to dig into my cash stash and put Rs. 50,000 (about $500 US) in my pocket, just in case the Shahpur police wanted to give us a hard time and demand a bribe.

The only stop I wanted to make besides mandatory bathroom breaks was to get some gas and pick up some snacks before hitting the road. I was becoming more and more concerned about my father's condition with every passing hour, and I wasn't going to drag the trip out. I blasted music most of the way to keep myself awake, while the constable snored in the backseat. Ali tried his best to keep me company, but he, too, succumbed to sleep, leaving me to pry my weary eyes open and stay on the road on my own.

It was still dark when we pulled into the station around 6:30

---

[1] Unfortunately, Officer Bashir was transferred to another location toward the end of 2016.

a.m. There was no one around except one officer that I did not know. I peeked into my father's room. He clutched a skimpy blanket to himself, curled on his bed like a child. The sight hurt my heart.

We asked the officer on duty to call the SHO. He hesitated, not wanting to bother his senior that early in the morning, I insisted. The SHO didn't pick up his phone. I went to sit with my father, who was now awake and eager to hear about all we had done in Islamabad.

"Did you talk to Abbas?" he asked. "Did he help you?"

I had to tell him the truth—that Abbas had not even bothered to call me back, let alone help. If my father was disappointed, he did not show it.

He was hungry, but we had to find some light food that wouldn't upset his injured stomach. So Ali, the constable, and I went out to look for a good breakfast place. Nothing was open before eight. While we circled the city, my phone rang. It was my wife. I got out of the car to talk with her in private. She had been in constant panic mode since my arrival in Pakistan, and her voice was high and urgent in my ear. I told her we had reached Shahpur safe and sound and expected to take my father back home that day.

After I hung up, we restarted our fruitless search for an open restaurant. Then I had an idea. I headed toward the hotel we had stayed at, thinking of the cook there who had made a wonderful breakfast for us the day before. He was asleep when we arrived, but he graciously got up and agreed to cook a nice breakfast for us. We ordered extra for the officers waiting back at the station, too.

The station had filled up a bit by the time we arrived. My inspector friend greeted us with a smile. The policemen were happy to eat a hearty breakfast, but my father did not eat much. I had brought a lot of yogurt for him, which was the only thing he was able to eat, but he didn't seem to want it. He was still suffering from diarrhea, having to go to the bathroom again and again. This concerned me, especially because we would be on the road for hours, and bathroom availability is scarce along the highways in Pakistan.

After eating his breakfast, my father called Ali and I to him. He looked in our eyes and began to cry.

"I am at my breaking point!" he said, his voice strained and tenuous. "I do not want to fight with anyone anymore. My wealth has become my enemy."

I tried to calm him down; reminding him that he was still alive, which was more than enough to be happy about. I reassured him that he would be getting medical treatment soon and would be in good health once again. After that, he could carry on with his life as before.

Shahpur "car address"

After finishing breakfast, we did not have to wait long before the SHO arrived. He had a short meeting with his staff and then he called me into his office along with the inspector.

"Syed, I told you to bring an inspector. Why did you bring a constable?"

I was dumbfounded. "We just worked until two in the morning to get this FIR done," I said, trying to contain my anger. "There was no inspector available. The Kohsar SHO called and confirmed that a constable would be all right. I don't understand."

"I made no such agreement," he said with a level look.

I could not believe it. The conversation had taken place in front of me!

"It isn't in my power to make an agreement like that," he said. "Those orders came directly from the DCP. There isn't much I can do."

I tried again, reminding him of my father's deteriorating health condition, but he flatly refused to release my father into the custody of a constable.

"There are many inconsistencies in the FIR, too," the inspector said matter-of-factly. "They forgot to mention that your father was intoxicated when he was arrested, and they failed to adequately describe the condition he was recovered in."

I stared at them both, feeling somewhat betrayed. I was utterly exhausted. It had been about eighty-eight hours since I'd had a sound sleep.

How many people do you know who can think straight after eighty-eight hours of restlessness?

Trying my best to hide my anger, I continued to negotiate, but my demeanor was now changing from one of cooperation to one of frustration. When I started raising my voice to the police, Ali pulled me aside and asked me to follow him outside to the car. Arguing with the police in Pakistan brings nothing but trouble, so Ali got me out of there before I could do any real damage. Our constable friend from Islamabad followed us.

"What's going on? Why are they going back on everything?" I asked, throwing my hands in the air in anger.

"I think it's time for a bribe," was the constable's blunt reply. "Making up fake issues is a common tactic used to prompt a payment."

Ali and I thought that bribery was unfair since we had met all the agreed upon demands, not to mention all the hassle the additional trip to Islamabad had caused us. Perhaps we could have understood their desire for a bribe if they had bent some rules and let my father go the day before, but not now, after we had gone through all the appropriate channels. Was releasing a suspect to a constable really an issue for the SHO, or was he, as the constable suggested, just looking to siphon a bribe from us?

Then I remembered a book I had read titled *Winning through Intimidation* by Robert Ringer, a real estate broker. The book contains an anecdote from when he was involved in a lawsuit. A client in faraway town had refused to pay him an agreed upon commission based on a technicality. When a negotiation with the other party's attorney was going nowhere, he brought in a local attorney to help him. The two locals were able to reach a consensus much easier. The author calls this "attorney-to-attorney respect law," which dictates that when two parties from the same profession sit down to talk, they typically have more respect for each other and thereby come to an agreement much faster.

Therefore, I thought if the constable had a candid conversation with the Shahpur police about what their real motivations were, they might be more prone to open up to him than us.

It worked.

"You were right," he said, sliding back into the car a few minutes later. "They want payment and then they will release your father. If they don't get the money, they'll keep bringing up my rank and complaining about made-up errors in the FIR."

"It's not going to happen!" said Ali, furious. "We met all their demands. Now they must live up to their promise and let Mubashar go!" He fumed for a moment before saying, "Maybe we should go back to the DCP."

Then I gave a speech while still on the driver's seat, which would go as Shahpur car address in history.

"Yes, Ali, we've done everything police asked and they are being unfair, but don't forget how precarious a position we're in here. Dad is in bad shape, and we need to get him treatment fast. You understand that better than anyone else here, don't you?" He nodded, and I kept going. "Go back to the DCP? You saw what kind of a guy he is. He didn't believe Dad's story at all. You really think he'll just say, 'Oh, no problem,' when he finds out that we didn't bring an inspector like he asked? If you ask me, we should avoid him altogether." I looked to the constable. "You can go ahead and let them know we're willing to work with them, but if we do this, they have to let my dad go right away! No more delays."

"But…" Ali began, but then his shoulders slumped as he looked at me. I'm certain the image of my father on that shabby bed was in his mind then. "Alright."

To my surprise, the constable told us that the force had already discussed the bribe and had decided to divide the funds in order of rank—the SHO would get the most, the inspector the second highest amount, then the sub-inspector, etc. They had already gone so far as to perform a headcount to determine how the money would be distributed.

When everything was all said and done, we paid Rs. 20,000 ($200 US) to appease everyone.

Now that doesn't seem like too large a sum to a westerner, but keep in mind that the SHO of a rural town like Shahpur probably only makes about Rs. 20,000 per month. His cut of around Rs. 5,000 would have been a good chuck of money for him. The same would hold true for the other officers.

After the constable delivered the funds, he returned with a smile on his face and said that the inspector was calling me inside. Ali was to stay behind. As soon as I entered the room, the inspector greeted me warmly before inviting me outside to sit at a table in the open air while he penned a report "to my liking." I asked him to just write the truth, and we would be fine. He spoke aloud while he wrote, for transparency.

While I sat listening, I thought to myself that "money magic" really does work in Pakistan.

CHAPTER 07

THE LONG JOURNEY HOME

By around 11 a.m. on February 18, 2016, we left Shahpur at long last. The police released my father's car into our custody, so I drove it with my father while Ali drove his with the constable. My father sat in the back so that he could lie down if he wanted. It wasn't the smoothest drive. My father's car is a stick shift, and I had to overcome a steep learning curve very quickly, as I'm used to automatics. Still, I took the lead because I had some reservations about Ali's driving skills.[2]

We stopped near the city of Bhera after driving for about an hour and a half. My father was hungry and needed the bathroom. The city harkened back to ancient civilizations… or at least the eighteenth century. Instead of taxis, *tongas*—the Pakistani word for horse-drawn buggies—rolled down the streets looking for fares. For those feeling fancy, rickshaws, which are basically scooters tied to a small cabin—peddled rides, too. I had a hard time finding any restaurants that looked halfway decent but at last discovered one that looked reasonably classy.

---

[2] Later, when we reached Islamabad, the constable joked about Ali's driving skills and how he made him nervous multiple times along the way.

I ordered some *daal* (lentils) and *naan* (bread) and delivered them to the cars. We ate quickly, as my most immediate goal was to get my father to the hospital as soon as possible. My father finished up his meal in the back as I drove. Soon after, he had to take his medication. We had barely started driving again before Dad had to go to the bathroom. It's not always easy to find a bathroom in these rural areas, and though I searched, I came up empty. My father insisted it was urgent, so I had to stop the car by the side of the road and let him relieve himself behind an abandoned building. Ali and the constable waited behind us. It was difficult to watch my father go through this, and it only fueled my anger and resentment toward the criminals responsible.

Next came the Motorway, where the driving would become relatively easy. However, my father's need to repeatedly go to the bathroom concerned me. The Motorway is built similarly to US highways; there are a limited number of exits and not all of them have restrooms. Most problematic was the mountain range between Bhera and Islamabad. Ali's car had made the trip just fine, but I was a bit worried about the condition of my father's car and its ability to climb the steep grade. It was a 2005 model Suzuki Cultus, and the stick shift had grown stiff, making it hard to switch from one gear to another. The engine made struggling noises whenever I tried to accelerate to pass slow-moving vehicles.[3] This mountain range is the most dreaded portion of the Motorway, and you routinely see many stranded vehicles along the shoulder. Basically, your car has to be in a tip-top shape to cross this mountain range gracefully.

---

[3] My father had a much nicer car, a Toyota Sedan that was like new, but the kidnappers had chosen to steal this one. I believe they thought this old clunker car would make their planned staged car accident death seem more believable.

Dad, our car just broke down

The first part of the Motorway drive went by without a hitch, but then the mountains loomed. As soon as we began the steep ascent, I felt the car revolt. The engine whined. I shifted from fifth gear to fourth to keep the car going. Pretty soon I had to shift into third. The car's engine wheezed, and the steering wheel vibrated in my hand. Then I was in second. The car continued to slow until we were only traveling about 20km/hr (12mph). The grade became steeper, and I knew my car was coming to a screeching halt. I shifted into first and headed toward the shoulder, where the car came to a complete stop. The engine chugged on, but each time I pressed the gas, the engine howled in protest, and the car never budged.

We were stranded in the middle of nowhere.

Ali pulled up behind me, and he and the constable hopped out to see what had happened. After I explained that the car kept slowing down no matter how hard I accelerated and that now it wouldn't even budge, the constable said, "You probably burned out the clutch plate, pushing the engine hard like that." Unfortunately, though he was something of a handyman, he couldn't fix it himself. He said it was no menial job; it required a workshop and an experienced mechanic.

Another uphill battle!

This breakdown was the last thing I was hoping for. Exhausted, unable to think straight, I stood by the side of the highway just watching the passing traffic, at a loss for what to do.

"I need to go to the bathroom," my father said.

We all looked at the open highway. No bathrooms in sight. He moved into some nearby bushes and relieved himself. Watching that reminded me of his total misery that only made me feel more helpless. I was close to giving up.

I sat at the wheel and asked Ali and the constable to do something; I was tired of making the decisions. Ali dialed 15, the equivalent to 911 in the US, and was told that he should walk about fifteen to twenty minutes northbound, and he would reach a public phone booth. He should dial the number for highway tow services from there, and they would come to our aid. Ali hung up and started walking, his tired feet dragging up the hill. I watched him, my eyelids drooping from fatigue, until he disappeared around a sharp turn.

I think I must have dozed for a while when a loud honk abruptly woke me. I turned around and looked at my father, who was resting in the back seat with eyes closed. Then I looked out the front and saw Ali walking toward us.

"Someone from the tow service is on his way," he said.

"How long?" I asked.

"Twenty, twenty-five minutes. At least that's what they said."

To our amazement, the tow truck drivers arrived on time and were very efficient in loading the car. I stayed in the car while it was towed and actually took a picture from inside, which you can see below.

Actual photo I took from inside my car while it was being towed. The car is sitting on the bed of the truck. (Date: February 2016, Source: Author)

My father got in Ali's car, and they and the constable followed right behind the tow truck. The sun had started to go down by the time we reached the workshop.

The workshop was of reasonable size, and it seemed like the mechanic had the expertise to fix the car. Like the constable, he was rather quick to diagnose the clutch plate as the problem after hearing my story. He explained that when a car engine is taxed too much by something like driving uphill for prolonged periods of time, the clutch plate burns up due to excessive overheating inside the engine. He initially quoted Rs. 10,000 ($100 US) for the work, but after some negotiation, he agreed to Rs. 8,000 ($80 US). There was no more time to bargain, plus there was no one else to fix it anyway, so I asked him to go ahead and do the job.

As a side note for those of you who wish to visit any Asian country, understand that everything is negotiable there—except for necessities like food and gas. Prices are often jacked up anyway because the vendors expect that customers *will* negotiate them down. If you visit Pakistan or any other Asian country, and you are not prepared to bargain, you are setting yourself up for a rip-off.

While the mechanic worked, we walked to a restaurant attached to a truck stop down the road. It was not too classy, but clean and comfortable enough to enjoy a meal. We didn't order much food; we were really just killing time. I hardly ate, but I made sure to drink a lot of bottled water. In Pakistan, you never want to drink tap water, because the water supply is not clean. Tap water is the surest way to get diarrhea. Thank God I didn't get diarrhea during those numerous trips from Shahpur to Islamabad; I would have been miserable.

After we finished eating, we went back to the workshop, but the car still wasn't ready. We made ourselves as comfortable as we could in the provided customer chairs outside the shop. During the wait, my father struck up a conversation with me about his newfound tenant and friend, Abbas. He reiterated that Abbas was a very nice guy and that I should ask his assistance again as soon as we got back home. Although I listened patiently, I still had some reservations about Abbas being my father's "good" friend. For one, he'd never bothered to call me back, let alone meet up to help out with police matters in Islamabad. Second, he'd technically lied to my father when he said he would help me but never did. Please don't get me wrong, I was not at all hurt for myself by his absence. As a matter of fact, I did all right without his help. My hurt originated from the fact that my father had been somewhat abandoned and betrayed (at least in my opinion) by a man he considered a sincere friend. I guess my definition of a sincere friend is very different from my father's. If I had been kidnapped and left on death's door, a person I considered a good friend would leave everything in the world to come to my aid. Nothing would be more important to him than helping me out of that difficult situation. However, I did not have the heart to argue with my father, at least not at that time, so I just kept quiet.

The mechanic completed the repairs around 6 p.m. Darkness was already falling, so I paid quickly, and we headed out. Unfortunately, I later found out that this mechanic actually screwed us. He had done a half-ass job, and after a month or so, the car broke down again. I guess he figured that people only came to him after highway breakdowns, so the majority of his customers were out-of-town folks who would never return to complain. Needless to say, it was a rip-off.

We drove straight to Pakistan Institute of Medical Sciences after entering Islamabad, and we arrived at the entrance gate around 8:30 p.m. As a doctor over there, Ali was familiar with admission procedures, and he mentioned to my father that the hospital staff would ask him if it was a regular admission or a medico-legal case (MLC). An MLC is a case of injury or ailment in which investigations by law-enforcement agencies are essential in pinning down the parties responsible for the injury or ailment.

"Do you want to register it as an MLC?" Ali asked.

I was surprised by the question. It was obvious to me that, as a criminal case requiring police involvement, it could hardly be registered as anything but. My father agreed, and once inside, he was taken directly to the emergency room where he was quickly examined and admitted to the hospital as an MLC.

By that time, I had endured about ninety-eight hours of almost nonstop misery, and my memory of the admission process and all the paperwork remains vague due to being dead tired at the time. I couldn't believe how much had happened in just three days, and my body seemed to be shutting down due to extreme fatigue. My eyes burned, and I couldn't focus. I was sure if I didn't rest, I risked facing some illness brought on by sheer exhaustion (maybe passing out on the cold hospital floor or slipping into a comma). The only thing I remember clearly about the hospital is the last glimpse of my father as they took him away. His eyes seemed to silently thank me, although I had done nothing more than what any responsible and loving son would do. There was hope in his eyes, and he looked more relieved than ever now that he was in a doctor's hands. I stepped forward and hugged him.

"You're out of danger now, Dad," I said in his ear. "Things will only look up from here."

Then I was walking with heavy feet toward Fiza's home, which was only a few minutes away.

Sometimes I wish there was a global contest in which winners were chosen based on the number of days they could carry on without restful sleep. I am confident that I'd have a good chance of being the winner. Add in enduring the misery of dealing with a loved one's kidnapping, and I don't think I would even have a contender. If you know someone who has gone through a similar misery, please do not hesitate to contact me, and I will give you a gift to deliver as my kudos to them.

It must have been around 11 p.m. on February 18, 2016, when I crashed on my bed and fell into a deep sleep thinking that the worst was over.

If only I had been right.

CHAPTER 08

WATCH YOUR BACK

My father would remain in the hospital for the next ten days, but there was no time for me to just sit and wait around. The first thing I had to do was get inside the house and gauge the extent of the damage and looting the kidnappers had done. But entering the house without the police would have been a terrible mistake. I worked it out so that the police force would accompany me when I entered for the first time. This arrangement took some time, though, and during the interim, my father had started to insist that his personal assistant, Peter, and I should just break into the house. It was his residence, after all, and he proclaimed that he had every right to get inside without anyone else's permission. He even asked Peter to climb the wall and break the locks. The police did not give a hoot if we entered the home or not, but breaking in was the only option because the kidnappers had stolen my father's keys. Peter came to Ali and me outside my father's hospital room, asking what he should do about the request. I told him that my father was not thinking clearly and breaking into the house without the assistance of authorities would just open a nasty can of worms down the road. If future litigation ensued, the opposing party could argue that because we went inside, we'd tampered with the evidence, or worst yet, suggest we planted it ourselves. Ali and I told Peter to ignore Dad's wishes for the sake of his case. Peter understood what we were saying, but he was scared to ignore a direct request from his boss. He wanted our assurance that he would not be fired or get into any trouble. I told him I would take full responsibility for ignoring Dad's wishes, and assured Peter he didn't have to worry.

During negotiations with police, I lived at Fiza's place. Police finally said they were ready to get inside the house on February 22, 2016. I documented the day with my cell phone camera. Peter, the inspector, and I gathered outside the house, and Peter broke the lock of the front door while an inspector watched (see picture below). This inspector was the officer assigned to my father's case going forward, and my father and I would be working with him extensively during the upcoming months.

Getting inside my father's house for the first time after his kidnapping. You can see yours truly reflected in the window. Peter is pictured on the right breaking the lock while the inspector, pictured on the left, acts as a witness. (Date: February 2016, Source: Author)[4]

---

4   After publishing this book, I envision having an exhibition where I could display all

My father's ransacked room (Date: February 2016, Source: Author)

---

these pictures for an audience and maybe invite a few movie producers from both Hollywood and Bollywood and make a movie based on this real life experience of mine.

Peter went through the home and broke all the entry locks while the rest of us examined the damage. It looked like a bomb had exploded in my father's room. It was completely ransacked. Papers, binders, albums, and even bed-sheets blanketed the floor. As we tried to walk through the room to figure out what had been taken, the tinkle of glass underfoot signaled broken picture frames tossed aside like trash. The floor crunched as we moved. Important documents were scattered and ripped. The desk drawers were hanging open like mouths forced to vomit up their contents. The top of the desk was littered with anything the burglars had deemed uninteresting.

The forensics team was on another job and running late. It was about 4 p.m. when the fingerprint squad finally showed up and started to attempt to lift prints. All the items were in disarray, and the team combed over them, trying to find ones that seemed to have been touched by intruders. Sadly, they could not find a single fingerprint worthy of recording. I looked in the closet where my father had all his property title documents (called registries), his Pakistani passport, his Green Card, and everything thing else of importance, and it was completely empty. The kidnappers had snatched my father's life's work away from him.

After the police finished their investigation, I asked the locksmith Peter had hired to change the locks on all the doors of the house. After that was done and the police had left, I went back to the hospital and broke the news to my father that all his property title documents, his and Fiza's passports, his checkbooks, and his cash were, indeed, gone. He didn't appear shocked—he'd been expecting it—but he sighed, and his face drew down in sorrow.

Shades of "The Godfather"

We had some extremely stressful days ahead of us. Fiza and I were sick with worry about our father's continued safety, and the same questions continued to plague our minds. The most frightening thing about Dad's kidnapping was that we had no idea who we were up against. In other words we did not know who the culprits were and what were they capable of. However, what was given was whoever they were, they must have known by then that "Mr. Mubashar" had survived and was recovering at PIMS hospital.

What would be their next step? Would they attempt to finish the job and send someone to kill our father in his hospital bed? If they did, there would be little protection. The hospital room doors were never locked, and locking them from the inside was against policy, because nurses always needed access to the patients.

What if we all stayed with him in his room? Would the assassin(s) kill us, too?

Was it possible they could bribe a nurse and put poison in his food?

No matter how paranoid it may sound, all those concerns were completely legitimate, given the awful circumstances we'd found ourselves in. Worried we were overthinking things, Fiza and I called our brother Ijaz in Australia to ask his opinion. Instead of soothing our doubts, he told us that we had made a huge mistake by bringing our father back to Islamabad to begin with. He said we should have taken him to some distant city, like Lahore or Karachi, so that nobody would know where he was except us. He said we had to put ourselves in the kidnappers' shoes and think from their perspective.

"Imagine if you were a kidnapper and the man you attacked has escaped; your main goal would be to kill that person, period!" he said, raising the hair on the back of my neck.

"You're kidding yourselves if you think the kidnappers don't already know his room number," Ijaz went on. "He shouldn't be in a local hospital. He's relatively helpless. Plus, PIMS is the first place they would have checked."

He went on to say that it was still not too late to take Dad to a distant city and make his whereabouts unknown to the world.

Before he hung up, he asked, "You remember in *The Godfather* when they came to shoot the Godfather in his hospital room?"

"Yes, but why on Earth are you bringing that up right now?"

"Well, this is no different," said Ijaz. "Stay tuned for the sharp shooter to arrive any time now and put Dad in his crosshairs."

Needless to say, Fiza and I were in a state of complete panic by the time we hung up. Just as we'd begun to recover from the turmoil of the last three days—sinking once again into feelings of security and semi-normalcy—Ijaz sent us spinning one hundred and eighty degrees. If he was right, the worst was *not* behind us. Fiza and I put our heads together and tried to gauge the real danger as opposed to the perceived risk. We agreed that Ijaz did have a point, but we also agreed that it would be impossible to transfer Dad to another hospital now, let alone another city. Our father had barely started to recover from his near death experience and did not have the energy to even go to the bathroom by himself. Hauling him off to another city would only exhaust him further. Besides, he was in the middle of serious medical treatment, which seemed to be working. Most importantly, when we proposed the transfer to him, he outright refused and showed no signs of changing his mind.

I also ran the idea of a transfer by Ali, and though he agreed that Ijaz's security concerns were valid, he also rejected the idea. Our father was receiving first class treatment at PIMS, and Ali personally knew all the key doctors. This insider relationship meant that senior level doctors went out of their way to visit my father multiple times a day. All the staff members were extra attentive, too, because Ali was their superior. When all of this and my father's own wishes to stay put were taken into account, the idea of taking him somewhere else quickly lost steam.

Though the matter was settled, Fiza and I couldn't help talking the situation over some more when we returned to her home that night. She made a reference to another movie, a Bollywood film called *Baazigar* (English: Gambler). In the film, a very wealthy businessman's trusted partner obtains his signature via trickery and then evicts his wife and children from their own home while the businessman goes out of the country on a business trip. Later the businessman dies of heart attack from the shock, and the manager claims all his property. The parallels to our current situation couldn't be ignored. It seemed to us that the kidnappers had tried to kill our father and make it look like a natural death. If their plan had succeeded, would they have tried to lay claim to our family's property. At that point, God only knew what they'd had in mind… but the answers would come.

Though a transfer was now out of question, our father's security was still important to us. To tell you the truth, whole family's security had become an issue by now. And if you're thinking this is far-fetched, some criminals had killed a doctor just a couple of months before *inside* PIMS hospital. Our security quickly became the most pressing issue on our minds.

The more I thought about our situation and what could have

happened if our father had died while driving that car, the sicker to my stomach I became. Feelings of anger and helplessness battled inside of me. Although, on one hand, I was thankful to God that the worst had not transpired, on other, I was becoming aggrieved that this was happening to us at all. I wondered who was so furious with our father and, indirectly, our family that he or she would want to destroy us in this fashion. Second, who was smart enough to pull this off? The criminals had dotted all *i*'s and crossed all *t*'s. They had obtained Dad's thumbprints and signatures on blank stamp papers, which would later have been verified as genuine by all government agencies. The kidnappers would have become legal owners of our father's entire estate, leaving us either with nothing or fighting lawsuits for the rest of our lives. And given how things work in Pakistan, we children would have given up the fight sooner rather than later. But their planned had failed. My father had survived. Now they had to clean up the mess and try to get away free.

PIMS had its own security, but it was nothing impressive. Though, there was always a PIMS guard with a gun stationed at the front entrance of the building, someone concealing a weapon of their own could probably walk right past him. We were in a highly precarious situation, and it appeared that if we wanted security measures, we would have to arrange them ourselves using our own resources.

Strict safety precautions enforced

In light of the above, we worked out the following security precautions:

- The family would never visit Dad all at once—only one family member at a time.

- We would avoid visiting during normal visitation hours because those were posted all over the hospital. Instead, we would visit randomly and sporadically so that no one could anticipate when we would show up.

- Visits would be kept short, and we would always ask a hospital security guard or a family member to stand outside the room and watch for anyone suspicious.

- We would hire our own security guard whom we would station just outside of our father's room 24/7. Only approved family members and hospital personnel would be allowed inside.

When Fiza and I ran our safety measures by Ali, he immediately rejected the idea of having our own hired security guard, as the hospital did not allow personal security, especially not armed security. PIMS already had a contract with a security company (as most hospitals in Pakistan now do), which stations its own armed security personal at each entry point. Guns are not allowed inside the hospital, period, so stationing our own security guard with gun outside our father's room was out of the question. So, we gave up that idea, but we implemented all the other precautions immediately.

Next we had to deal with the safety and security of the family *outside* the hospital. I suggested to my father that we contact a security company who could help us make sure that we knew what to do should someone try to harm us. He thought I was overreacting, but I got in touch with the top security company in Islamabad, Phoenix Security, anyway. They invited me to their facility to educate me on how to be safe and "non-kidnappable." I had never heard that one before.

I got a kick out of the word, but they used it as official term during our conversation. The security company was located in the Blue Area, a large business district in Islamabad. I was greeted by a female receptionist who asked me to have a seat while I waited for the supervisor. He arrived shortly and ushered me upstairs, through a hallway, and into a more private office. It seemed that they were doing some renovations in that section of the building, and he apologized to me for the mess. We at last settled in a room with a large conference table. When his superior arrived, the two of them gave me a security briefing on how to be secure and make sure that I was not targeted or kidnapped by the criminal group after my father.

"How important do you think it is to carry a cell phone around to be able to make an emergency call?" the security guard asked as soon as we settled down to talk.

"I think it's pretty important to carry a cell phone at all times, given the situation we are in."

"Wrong! The biggest mistake you can make is to carry your cell phone around, thinking it's your best friend. It's your worst enemy."

"Why?"

"It gives away your location. Any operator at the cell phone company can pinpoint you within ten feet of your current position. A cell phone is a kidnapper's favorite tool for following victims."

"If a cell phone operator has to do it, how can the kidnapper find my location?"

"Simple... Bribery."

In a country such as Pakistan, where an experienced cell phone operator makes Rs. 20,000 ($200 US) a month (yes, per *month*) at most (the average is more like $120–$160), offering a $200 bribe for disclosing the location of a cell phone creates a serious moral dilemma for the operator. If he accepts, it would take him less than a minute to earn a full month's salary. All he needs to do to get it is dole out information that is readily accessible on his computer screen. And kidnappers provide steady work, at least until they are successful in their kidnapping attempt. Sometimes the temptation is too great.

Now, I am not saying that all operators are corrupt. However, considering that there are about one hundred operators in a single shift, the likelihood of finding one susceptible to bribery is very high.

The harsh reality is that bribery culture remains rampant in Third World countries. Salaries are too low to make a good living, and the gap between the haves and have-nots is too wide. Very often, bribers offer these low-paid employees the equivalent of their full month's salaries, if not more. Plus, the possibility of being caught is not that great. Take our corrupted operator, for instance. How is an employer supposed to catch one employee hidden within three shifts of one hundred operators, each, just within twenty-four hours of operations? It only takes a moment for someone to secretly divulge location information to outside parties. It is almost impossible for a supervisor to catch. The only way these operators typically get caught, really, is if their equally under-paid coworkers find out *and* tell on them.

"Only use your cell phone while driving or when you are sure that you are not going to be in any one place for more than a few minutes," the Phoenix Security employee told me. "Turn it off fifteen minutes before you arrive at any destination where you will be stationary for longer periods of time, like eating at a restaurant."

He explained that turning it off at the restaurant was too little too late; a malicious party would already know my location. If they saw that you were at a place such as a restaurant, they would also know that you were going to be there for a while.

They also told me to sleep at different places if possible.

"Go sleep at a friend's house one night and your sister's house another. And don't fall into a routine with your sleeping places, either. Don't get into any routines for that matter. Don't leave or come back to the house at the same time every day. You *must* change it up, especially if you are staying at a familiar location like your father's house for longer periods of time."

As far as the security of my father was concerned, they were alarmed to hear that he planned to go back to the same home he was kidnapped from. They told me point blank that it would be the most unwise decision possible. They suggested he stay in a guest-house, at a friend's house, or anywhere else; he should not permanently stay in his own home. Later when I tried to convince my father of the wisdom in this, he refused to move anywhere else. He said that everyone had to die one day, and if his time was meant come in his own home, so be it.

Below are the verbatim instructions the security company provided for our father's safety and ours.

Safety Procedures

- Physical security of the subject (my father) is of utmost importance

- Subject's location should be known to as few people as possible

- Ensure security is present during his hospital stay
- Ensure security is present when he is discharged from the hospital
- If the subject decides to go back to live in the house he was kidnapped from, he should have proper security outside the house, 24/7
- The subject should even consider a personal bodyguard to accompany him at all times, even while performing daily life functions
- Consider letting go of all previous employees, even if they were once trusted
- Do not discuss your travel plans and movements in public areas where these can be overheard
- Power off all cell phones while not in use
- As a last resort, carry a gun, but consult an attorney first

These instructions raised alarm bells for us all, and we were on high alert as a precaution. Basically, we were watching our backs *all* the time.

CHAPTER 09

MEET OUR ATTORNEY: MR. IQBAL

Over the next few days, my father continued to recover, albeit slowly. His bowels were in the worst shape. He had constant diarrhea and continuous urges to go to the bathroom. Despite these issues, he was well taken care of by the hospital staff, which was comforting, and it seemed like he was getting better one day at a time.

When my father had been in the hospital for three or four days, I started visiting with him for short periods of time each day to get his thoughts on how I should proceed with his case. Back at the house, though the locks had been replaced, I still did not think it was a good idea to live there, but I had asked Peter go check on the place every day. I made some rounds myself several times a day, but I was still not ready to sleep there, at least not until my father was discharged from the hospital.

Somehow, I had become the one in charge of taking care of all his affairs, even though I was a foreigner. Of course, it helped that I had grown up in Pakistan, so I adjusted to the flow of things easier than most.

At the time, the main concern with the case was that Islamabad Police still had not recorded my father's official statement. For days, they called on me asking to set up a time to get it done, but I wanted my father to feel better before police talked with him. Furthermore, I did not want his statement recorded without an attorney present.

Our attorney's introduction

It must have been either February 24 or 25 when my father invited an attorney to the hospital. The attorney's name was M. Kokab Iqbal, and he was a renowned lawyer in Islamabad. His title on his business card was "Advocate, Supreme Court of Pakistan." Not all attorneys can represent clients in all courts. There is a particular seniority level, along with credentials, that they must obtain before they can represent clients in the Supreme Court, like Mr. Iqbal. In Pakistan, attorneys start their careers representing in lower courts, and as they move up, they are assigned to higher courts. You are not qualified to represent in the Supreme Court of Pakistan unless you've reached a senior level. Therefore, there was no doubt in my mind that my father had retained a good attorney. Mr. Iqbal was an elderly gentleman in his 70s. He wore thick glasses and sported the typical uniform attire of an attorney in Pakistan: black coat, black tie, white shirt, and khaki pants. I guess there is some leeway in the color of the pants, but they definitely need to be light.

Mr. Iqbal arrived in the room with his secretary, who had all the files tucked firmly under his elbow. He walked very slowly, and his posture was slightly tilted to one side. He was soft spoken and seemed to think through every sentence before he spoke. If there was ever a stereotypical senior attorney, this was him. As soon as he arrived, I thought we ought to go ahead and get the statement out of the way. I had built some rapport with the police at the Kohsar station, namely SHO Bashir and some of his staff, so I called them up and told them my father could now record a statement.

Dealing with Pakistani police is quite a chaotic experience that could easily drive a westerner bonkers. Now to be fair to Pakistani police, they are a resource-starved agency in already a poor country. With scarce funds, allocation of resources relies on lots of politics. Unlike other Third World countries, Pakistan has a history of maintaining a strong military force, and most of the tax payer money goes toward military spending. Schools come next, then hospitals, and lastly police and other government agencies. The funding is then further divided among the different police ranks: military police, the FIA (Federal Investigation Agency), the Rangers (paramilitary force), and the common police force, in order of importance.

The fact that the common police force is ranked at the bottom is an open secret in Pakistan. Common criminals take full advantage of this. As long as they can dodge common police, and don't do something serious enough to involve higher-ranking agencies, it is likely they won't be caught any time soon. High profile cases are never handed over to the regular police force, which is a shame. Instead, they go to the military police, which is far better trained, or the military itself. Pakistan military gets the lion's share of resources and even has a "secret budget," the amount of which is not disclosed to common citizens. The military force is kept strong because of the constant rivalry with neighboring India that began in 1947. Since then, India and Pakistan have fought three major wars over territory disputes regarding the region of Kashmir. So in the eyes of citizens, any expense for the military is completely justified, and since politicians have to obtain votes from those citizens, they let sleeping dogs lie. This lack of funding and respect makes it hard for the regular police to get things done in a smooth, organized fashion.

When I called the Kohsar station, hoping to get an officer over quickly to take a statement, or *biyan* in Urdu, I was told that the officer assigned to my father's case was out of town on another assignment. I asked why they couldn't just send someone else to fill his shoes and stop by. "We will see what we can do," was the only response I got. So I was not sure if the statement would be taken that day or not.

My father instead narrated his story to Mr. Iqbal, who listened patiently. At the end, my father told him that his main concern at that moment was to safeguard his property from being illegally transferred to the kidnappers because of the stamp papers. Stolen property title documents are an extra huge nightmare in a country like Pakistan. Reason being, there are no electronic records, so the only proof of ownership on a property are those title documents. Obviously my father's kidnappers had tried to take advantage of this weakness, risking themselves further to burglarize his house and steal those documents, even though they already had his prints and signatures. They knew that down the road, having the titles in hand would make proving that Mr. Mubashar had sold them all his property before his car accident much easier. I had no doubt in my mind we were dealing with some very clever criminals.

Mr. Iqbal said that since my father was still alive, it was highly unlikely that the criminals would ever try to transfer his property into their names (although he did not completely rule this out). He said if they did anything, they would most likely attempt to sell off his properties to multiple buyers at once!

In order to grasp what Mr. Iqbal was cautioning against, you have to understand the procedure for selling a property in Pakistan. In a process not too different from other parts of the world, a buyer pays upfront earnest money to the seller of the property with the guarantee that the buyer will pay the full balance once the title is transferred into his or her name. Mr. Iqbal explained that what these scoundrels typically do is interest many potential buyers in the same house. Obviously these potential buyers don't know each other, so the criminals collect earnest money from as many buyers as they potentially can for the same house and then, when the buyers show up for their titles, the criminals are nowhere to be found. As an example, imagine this scam being pulled on a house worth Rs. 50,000,000 ($500,000 US). Typically, 5% ($25,000) would be a reasonable amount to hand over as earnest money. Also, depending on the buyer, there is very little due diligence performed at this stage as to the transferability of the property, and buyer is mostly reliant on the seller's word regarding how long the transfer process is going to take. Say the seller is committing fraud against four potential buyers. That is $100,000 in his pocket, which is a hefty sum even in the US, let alone in a poor country like Pakistan. The kidnappers possessed the title documents of about eight or nine properties, and all they needed to do was pull this scam off a few times on each property to be comfortably wealthy for the rest of their lives.

What would the defrauded buyers do after they found out they had been ripped off? They would file a lien against the property, and a drawn out legal battle would ensue between the buyers and the real owners, a.k.a our family. We could try and explain that it was all a fraud, but the buyers would still want their earnest money back, and things can drag out in Pakistani courts for years. Throw into the equation the fact that most officials are corrupt, and the misery is multiplied several times. Being settled in the US with my family, and used to a streamlined system, I would neither have the time nor the stamina to carry out that mud wrestle and would give up on this legal nightmare sooner rather than later.

Many people have lost their property to crooks this way because they did not have the fortitude to stick it out in court for the rest of their lives, but more on that later.

Obtaining a stay order

A month ago, we might have considered this complex plot far-fetched, but then, a month ago we also would have laughed at the suggestion that Dad might be kidnapped. Mr. Iqbal suggested we immediately file petitions with all the courts in Islamabad to freeze transfers on all properties under my father's ownership. This is called a 'stay order'. After we had filed the order, we would need to forward it to the agency responsible for all property transfers in Islamabad, the Capital Development Authority (CDA). This would give us a dual advantage. Typically, buyers consult with courts before they buy a property or hand earnest money over to a seller. The courts would then inform the buyer of the stay order on file, which would be an immediate red flag that something was wrong with the transferability of this particular property. Furthermore, if these criminals were to line up a totally naïve buyer who still ended up paying them earnest money, a stay order filed with court would be our shield freeing us of legal responsibility. Filing it with CDA would further ensure that the property transfer to the new name would never be consummated unless that stay order is lifted, which again only courts can do.

Next, Mr. Iqbal gave us some advice on how to handle my father's criminal case.

- Make sure the official statement is recorded in front of a magistrate. I think he was suggesting this to avoid corrupt police officers changing anything in my father's statement.

- Seek help from some senior officials, such as the Senior Superintendent of Police (SSP) or even the Inspector General of Police (IG). If nothing else, our effort would make sure they knew that my father was a kidnapping victim, not a criminal.

- Request the help of the General of the Pakistan Military. A long shot, but worth taking because things get done in a hurry in Pakistan if the military gets involved.

In addition to recording a statement with the magistrate, we were advised to request a stop of transfer of property without my father's presence at the CDA and also request expedition of lower court matters from the Supreme Court of Pakistan, which is typically reserved only for foreigners. The idea is that if a foreigner is stuck in Pakistan due to unforeseen circumstances and must return to his country of nationality, he can ask for expedited processing through the courts and even with the police. In this case, I would be the foreign claimant asking for this service.

It may not look like an overly complicated to-do list, but when I left Pakistan on June 4, 2016, after four months of struggling to get these few things done, many of the items were still pending. That's how slow the system works in Pakistan.

My father's first official statement to Islamabad police

We were already a couple of hours into the meeting with our attorney, and there were still no signs of police. Mr. Iqbal was ready to leave. I again dialed the station, but there was no answer, so Mr. Iqbal left with his secretary. About ten minutes later, the police showed up in the hospital room. I asked my father what he wanted to do. He looked exhausted, but instructed me to call our attorney back. Mr. Iqbal and his assistant turned around and came back without complaint.

The two police officers were from the Kohsar station, which had jurisdiction over my father's house. An officer from PIMS also sat in on the meeting. I called Ali in, too, making a total of eight people present.

When my father told his story, complete with the horrendous details of the torture tactics used against him, even the police officers were dumbfounded. This was my first time hearing the whole tale in intricate detail, and I still remember standing right in front of my father's bed with Ali at my side. One police officer wrote down the statement, and Mr. Iqbal hovered over his shoulder, requesting corrections where he deemed fit. I regret not making a video recording of the statement as well. As I listened to the full story for the first time, my heart felt heavy as I realized the full extent of the torture my father endured. And for what? He had not harmed any of these kidnappers. Why had they tortured him like that? These criminals had tried to eradicate our well-known family name from Islamabad. After reading the chapters dedicated to our family biography, you will understand why this hurt the most—that someone had attempted to destroy our family's name and deprive legal heirs from the hard earned estate their parents had built over a lifetime. After the statement was in writing and everyone had disbanded, I went back to Fiza's feeling downtrodden. I shared the complete story with her.

She listened quietly but did not have much to say.

CHAPTER 10

TRUE RAGS TO RICHES STORY

After working his way up to Deputy Director in the early 1980s, my father had trouble advancing further in his government job. He was overlooked for promotion a number of times in favor of junior employees, and it did not sit well with him. So on a part-time basis, he started working with a friend of his who was involved in real estate sale and purchase. This friend would buy run-down houses, fix them up, and resell at a profit. He was involved in real estate brokerage also. Real estate licenses are not required to operate in Pakistan, so it was relatively easy to get involved in the business, especially part-time. This friend, Saeed Mughal, became a hero to my father, guiding him along the way to beginning and executing a successful business. Saeed Mughal was a rags-to-riches story in his own right, and thus my father had no qualms about becoming his protégé. I don't know whether it was thanks to his own instinct or upon Saeed's encouragement that my father decided to say goodbye to the government job and start his own business.

My father rented a modest space in walking distance from our townhome and started to operate from there as a real estate broker. Now for those of who are wondering about his leaving government job and a family to support, the good thing about government jobs in Pakistan is that they give you a lot of leeway. So in this case, my father actually did not quit his job but went on a five year leave, which was surprisingly allowed for a government officer at my father's scale at the time. Also another amazing thing is that the government does not immediately ask employees to vacate their government housing, and you can extend your stay almost up to five years.

Family fun on my father's motorbike

At this point in their lives, my parents did not own any transportation and had to take public transport. All my father owned was a bicycle. I have a memory of sitting on the front rod of that bicycle, taking a ride.

In 1981, after my father made a little progress in his real estate business, he was able to buy a motorcycle. It was a Honda 50CC, the smallest horsepower motorcycle one could get at the time and thus the cheapest. I was the only child at the time, and I was ecstatic when he first brought his motorcycle home, thinking about all the faraway places we could go on it. My first wish, promptly proclaimed to my parents, was to go to *Daman-e-Koh* (English: Foothills), a hill station about twenty-five minutes away from Islamabad. Daman-e-Koh is a viewing point on the Margalla Hills where people go for picnics and sightseeing. There is a restaurant up there that boasts a beautiful view of Islamabad from the dining area. Honoring my wishes, my parents got everything ready to take me to Daman-e-Koh on my father's brand new Honda 50CC. All three of us hopped on and headed for the foothills. There is only one main road that leads to this hill station. We cruised along it and passed by the Islamabad Zoo before the ascent up the foothills. When we started to the climb and the gradient became steep, the motorcycle slowed and started to struggle, but my father just gave it more throttle. We were almost halfway through our journey when the engine started growling. The ascent only became steeper, and the path took sharp turns. My father had to slow down around the turns and then crank the throttle to regain speed. I clearly remember feeling the engine come to a screeching halt, hearing it groan louder and louder each time my father twisted the throttle, and my dreamy excitement shattered and died with it.

My father did not give up so quickly, though. He had us sit patiently while the engine cooled, but when he again tried to climb the hill, the motorcycle stalled after moving only a few hundred meters. The 50CC engine just didn't have enough horsepower to climb that hill with three people aboard. Finally, my father made a U-turn and started the descent toward home. Surprise, surprise, the motorcycle did not have any problems coming down the hill. Alas! My dream of visiting Daman-e-Koh on my father's brand new motorbike was not going to be fulfilled after all. This is my sharpest memory of my father's first significant purchase.

When I was in Pakistan in 2016, I did manage to visit Daman-e-Koh and refresh some memories. That time, my car was powerful enough to get me to my destination. A selfie is included for your viewing below.

Your author at Daman-e-Koh (Date: May 2016, Source: Author)

A view of Islamabad from Daman-e-Koh
(Date: May 2016, Source: Author)

My father's first car purchase

My father kept working hard on his real estate business, and very soon he was able to hire his own employee, a man by the name of Jon. Jon was much older than my father, and he brought a lot of industry contacts with him. He also became a source of mature advice for my father. My father's business thrived in front of my eyes. I saw how hard he worked, and I watched as he became more confident. In two or three years, my father was able to afford a Suzuki FX.

My father standing proudly by his new car (Date: 1986, Source: Author's family albums)

This compact four-door sedan was a modest investment for a small family. By this time, both my brother and sister were already born. I was seven in 1984, and I remember the day the dealer dropped the car off at our townhouse in F-6. The only problem was that my father did not know how to drive. Without taking any lessons, he asked me to help him drive the car around town. I asked him if he was sure it was all right to do that, and he assured me that it would be fine. The car was parked on the front lawn. My father needed to get it in reverse and pull out onto the main thoroughfare that ran by our house. My father had nothing but some verbal instructions to guide him on how to operate a stick shift, but he was ready to dive into the venture. He rolled down the driver side window so that he could hear my instructions of when to keep going and when to stop as he worked to back off the lawn. I remember running beside the car as he drove down the main road, shouting orders to make sure he was driving straight. However, when he turned off the main road onto a side street, the gear got stuck. We had to ask a neighbor to come help us drive the car back home. It was a fun experience, and I got plenty of exercise that night. Most importantly, though, that car became a symbol to me of my father's climb to success.

My father's first major business deal

My father made swift financial progress in the mid-1980s, and he saved up some of that cash. He frequented vacant lot auctions, commonly referred to as plot auctions in Pakistan, held by the Capital Development Authority (CDA), which is a government agency that regulates land and property development. The CDA controls all aspects of property development including but not limited to zoning, building permits, building inspections, and enforcing adherence to codes. The CDA is a streamlined agency, and a piece of property under the CDA's jurisdiction garners a high level of trust. Any property under CDA control is automatically stamped as a clean title in the public eye. Getting a property with a clean title remains a challenge in many parts of the country thanks to greedy individuals and agencies ready to take advantage of faulty Pakistani law and order. Out-of-town buyers might purchase a piece of land and come back to find an occupied house built on it. Buyers can also run into scammers who sell the same property to ten different people, as we suspected my father's kidnappers might attempt to do. But if you purchase through the CDA, you get a clean title on a property that meets all city codes. It's a solid investment, and all properties sold by the CDA are situated within a jurisdiction with stricter law and order in place.

My father attended these CDA auctions to observe businessmen consummating property sale and purchase transactions. These were sharp people who knew what they were doing and who were making handsome profits in the process. Islamabad was a rapidly growing city at the time, and the CDA was selling a lot of land for development. My father made some wealthy friends at these plot auctions, and he convinced them of his own business acumen by advising them on a few transactions. His information was valuable to these out-of-towners because he had lived in Islamabad for quite a while and knew the city well. When my father expressed interest in taking part in these auctions himself, some of his wealthy friends agreed to lend him the money to do so. The way plot auctions work is that you put down a ten percent deposit to be allowed to bid on the auction. If you win the auction, you typically have two to three months to come up with the full payment to own the plot outright. But the market was so hot that people were actually able to sell their plots at a profit even before this two to three month time frame was even up, making a profit on their down payment alone. People were doubling their money in a few short months. You could put Rs. 20,000 down on a plot worth Rs. 200,000, and if a new buyer emerged who was willing to pay Rs. 220,000 for the plot before the full amount was due, you could sell the property, transfer the deed, and make a Rs. 20,000 profit—an astronomical rate of return by any standards anywhere in the world.

Though real estate in Islamabad has had its share of ups and downs, CDA property sales typically always remain a red hot market. Back in the 1980s, locals had the advantage because everything was done via snail mail. To save on expense, the CDA would send out mailers to only local citizens of Islamabad. Therefore, only these local citizens were privy to all the CDA auctions and could snap up property before resourceful people from neighboring towns got wind of them. When these outsiders wanted to buy land in Islamabad, they would have to buy it from locals. This led to a total real estate bonanza amongst locals with resources.

The only thing fresh-faced real estate brokers like my father had to be careful about was to not over-bid in excitement. If the price was too steep, it would be hard to turn the mortgage over to someone else within the CDA's two to three month timeframe, and you'd have to hold onto to it and make the full payment yourself.

The making of a businessman

In 1981, thanks to the connections he'd made by hanging around these plot auctions, my father scraped up Rs. 20,000 (about $1,200 US after inflation[5]) via loans and took part in an auction for a vacant piece of land worth about Rs. 200,000 ($12,000 US after inflation). Lo and behold, only a couple of months later, he found a buyer willing to pay Rs. 220,000 and doubled his money just like his new friends. Now my father had Rs. 40,000 in his pocket with which he could return the loan of Rs. 20,000, leaving him with Rs. 20,000 of his own money to play with. For those of you who are wondering,

---

[5] The exchange rates used throughout this manuscript are calculated using data tables from: http://nativepakistan.com/us-dollar-vs-pakistani-rupee-exchange-rates-since-1947/

According to these tables, the exchange rate of Pak Rs. vs US Dollar in 1986 was $1US = Rs.16.64. As of 2015, this ratio had ballooned to $1US = Rs. 102.77. This means there is a much higher rate of inflation in Pakistan. For current calculations, however, I have simply used $1US = Rs. 100 for the sake of simplicity throughout.

this is an astronomical return on investment (ROI) which equates to 400% annually (100% return in 3 months). If you consider that the money was borrowed and did not actually belong to my father, the ROI mathematically approaches *infinity*, considering his zero dollar upfront investment.

Over the course of the next three to four years, my father would repeat this process multiple times to accumulate a sum of Rs. 600,000 (about $36,000 US after inflation), a handsome sum in the early 1980s. While luck was certainly present in his success, the real key to his growth was his willingness to take educated risks. He left a secure government job in order to start on his own business, took a huge risk in securing a lease for the office space before he made any serious money, risked his government housing, and borrowed his first Rs. 20,000 for a deal that could have incurred a loss. But he had a knack for it, and his risks paid big. Any success story that I have ever heard or read about always has an element of risk, and my father's is no different.

My father never abandoned this method of business. In fact, just before he was kidnapped in 2016, he deposited a sum of Rs. 2,000,000 in order to purchase a plot in a CDA auction worth about Rs. 20,000,000, with a plan to sell it for profit in the next few months. The only difference between this transaction and the ones he used to do in '80s was that this time it was his own money. The market was still profitable all those years later.

Not even his kidnapping slowed him down. During my stay in Pakistan, I witnessed him sell this plot to a Swedish buyer for Rs. 20,600,000, earning a profit of Rs. 600,000. Though the market has slowed down somewhat in the forty years between today and his start—you cannot quite double your money anymore—for you mathematician types out there, making Rs. 600,000 on an initial investment of Rs. 2,000,000 in three months equates to an ROI of 120%. Where in the world except Pakistan can you get these types of returns on your original investment?

This particular business deal led to something that I consider to be a sign of God's hand in saving my father's hard-earned money. Because he had to deposit a sum of Rs. 2,000,000 with the CDA, this sum was no longer in my father's personal bank account when his kidnappers depleted his accounts.

Wow! I get goose bumps to this day just thinking about this. God does help in mysterious ways!

My father's purchase of his first house

With Rs. 600,000 in his pocket in 1984, my father stumbled upon a house priced well below market value. The house was on the market for only Rs. 800,000 ($48,000 US with inflation) even though the houses in that neighborhood were selling for around Rs. 2,400,000 ($144,000 US with inflation).

This house was labeled with a low price tag because it was subsidized by the government and allotted to a senior government employee who was paying rent that was far below the fair market prices at the time. To be exact, the government was paying about one third of the market value in rent to the owner at the time, but the actual reason the house was being sold for so cheap was because it was almost impossible in those days to evict a government employee from his house. This is a totally absurd practice, but that's how things used to work in Pakistan, and quite frankly, they have not changed much. The owner was stuck. The government was not going to increase the rent anytime soon, and suing the government would have been a massive waste of time and money. Evicting the tenant was out of the question, too.[6] Government employees are known to stay in government subsidized housing until they retire or die. The owner had tried for years to evict this government employee without any success, so he was selling the house for peanuts. He'd had enough.

My father knew that if he acquired this property, he might have a terrible time trying to kick out the tenant, but after he negotiated the price of a Rs. 2,400,000 house down to Rs. 600,000, he couldn't pass up the investment. He purchased his first house with no idea when (if ever) he would be able to live there, and he had some tough surprises in store for him in coming months.

The tenant had already been living there for quite a few years, and it didn't bother him much that the property had been acquired by a new owner. In his mind, he was going nowhere. My father knew he had gotten a bargain of a lifetime, but he underestimated how difficult it would be to kick this guy out. Right after the purchase, my father started the eviction process but immediately hit a brick wall. His biggest mistake turned out to be failing to realize that the real opponent was not the tenant, but the government itself. He submitted a lot of applications to the ministry where the tenant was employed, demanding he either vacate the premises or pay an increased rent of three to four times the current amount. The government officials who found these letters on their desks probably shared a few good laughs. My father got no response from the tenant or the government.

---

[6] Recall, a few years earlier, my father had continued to stay in a government subsidized townhome even after going on a leave of absence to start a business. Although my father had done nothing wrong legally, my point here is that the same system he once used to his advantage had now become his Achilles heels

My father tried meeting with senior government officers to try and convince them of the unfairness of having a permanent tenant paying about one third of standard market rent. My father told them that it was with his hard-earned cash that he had acquired this house, and if he could not ever live there, it would be a tragedy. As I understand, the government officials offered a lot of sympathy but not any concrete help.

My father also met in person with the supervisor of the tenant to make his plea directly, but to no avail. My father even pleaded directly with tenant over the phone. I vividly remember sitting in the tiny dining room of our townhouse in F-6 listening to my father plead with the tenant to move out due to the fact we would have to vacate our housing pretty soon since my father was no longer a government employee and the five year grace period was up. He reminded the tenant that he could easily get reasonable housing elsewhere, but that house was the only place my father had to move his growing family of five. Sometimes memories get imprinted on your mind forever. This was one such memory for me. My father's knees almost hit the floor. I saw his pain and heard the distress and aggravation in his voice, and I was old enough to realize that those feelings were caused by someone who was taking advantage of the screwed up system in Pakistan.

The tenant's main reason for not moving was that F-7 was an upscale neighborhood, and if the government gave him new housing, it would probably be in a lower class neighborhood because government housing had started to move out of the area. (By 2016, there wasn't a single government subsidized house in all of F-7.) That phone call was first time it really sank in for my father that perhaps this investment was more trouble than he had bargained for. He had already sunk all his hard earned money into this house from his earlier business dealings and now it seemed to turn out to be a big mistake.

After trying a bunch of different tactics over the course of almost two years, my father prepared his last resort, which, if it worked, had the best chance of kicking this tenant out. However, this tactic was a direct defiant act against the government, so if it failed, it would accrue serious resentment from the government, and my father would have to kiss any hope of getting his house back goodbye.

Meeting with Pakistan's military ruler, General Zia-ul-Haq

As his last ditch effort, my father planned to meet with the then current military ruler of Pakistan, General Zia-ul-Haq, who was assassinated a few short years later with a plane bomb on August 17, 1988. He is considered to be the most powerful ruler in Pakistan's history, ruling under martial law from 1977 to 1988. Martial law means that a military rule is imposed upon the country, suspending ordinary law, when the regular government is deemed dysfunctional. Martial law has been implemented multiple times in Pakistan since the country came into being in 1947. This military takeover is intended to be a short-term phenomenon in order to restore law and order, assist in carrying out new elections, and form a new stable government. Then the military typically gets out of the way of civilian government.

But in case of General Zia-ul-Haq, he came into power via military coup in 1977 with intentions of handing over rule to a civilian government but then changed his mind somewhere down the road and kept on imposing the military rule. As the saying goes, "Power tends to corrupt, and absolute power corrupts absolutely."

It took assassination to get General Zia-ul-Haq out of the way.

General Zia-ul-Haq, military ruler of Pakistan from 1977 to 1988. (Source: http://www.pakarmymuseum.com/exhibits/general-muhammad-zia-ul-haq-3/)

Going to see the general was a huge risk for my father. As soon as my father approached him, the government would be aware of his actions and would hold it against him. However, getting the general's absolute power behind him would almost guarantee a win. In any case, my father really didn't have much to lose. The government was not budging. He arranged a meeting with General Zia-ul-Haq in early 1986.

It was obviously not a piece of cake. Just landing the meeting took several months, and even then he was unsuccessful in getting an official face-to-face. All he got was an invite to a ceremony the general was going to attend. The idea was to try to solicit the general at the event. Rumor had it that the general typically allowed a few people to meet with him when he was at ceremonies. Usually his junior generals would pick and choose the people who were allowed to see him. The criterion for selection was unknown.

So, my father went to the ceremony, and after it was over, he waited for almost four hours just for a chance to see the general. It was also well known that the general might refuse meetings at the last minute, so there was no guarantee that he would honor any sort of meeting arrangement, no matter how many hours one had waited. Even if he decided he did want to meet people, his generals would choose them randomly.

As demonstrated by his budding business days, my father is pretty good at making friends on the fly and building rapport quickly. He started to talk with a junior general while he waited. He told him a little about his sad tale to gain his sympathy, hoping it would help sway the junior general in the selection process. After chatting with the junior, my father focused on how he would make his pitch to General Zia-ul-Haq in just ten minutes—the maximum allotted time per person.

As he whiled away time sitting in the waiting area, he thought about movie actors and how the best of them can leave an impression on an audience in a brief period of time. How long does an impassioned scene last? Not typically more than ten minutes and yet it can leave an audience bawling or cheering. What the actor is doing is not even real; it's just drama, an act. My father's situation was no made up act. Being deprived of his own home was his reality. My father asked himself, if an actor could make an impact with some made up scenes of hardship and heartache in just a few minutes, why could he not make an impact with the emotion from his own reality?

He thought about the struggles of his ancestors, how his mother and father migrated to Pakistan from India, and the sacrifices they had made for this country. He pondered his own struggles of working labor-intensive jobs as a child, graduating from college with limited financial resources, and finally scrapping enough money together to put a nice roof over his family's head only to find out that he couldn't live there because it was wrongfully occupied. My father's tongue itched to point out all these facts in front of the general, but his brain knew the most important thing would be his tone and the ability to convey and evoke strong emotion. After his emotional plea, he would present the general with a paper to sign, ordering the tenant and his employer (the government) to vacate the premises immediately.

This was all going to take some serious courage. There he was, a common citizen, planning to not only appear in front of the most powerful person in Pakistan at the time, but also to demand that he sign a paper with orders to kick out a government employee. It was a tall order.

Apparently his chat with the junior general had made an impact, because my father was selected. I think those ten minutes in front of the general were some of the most memorable moments of my father's life. Each time my father narrated this meeting in my presence (believe me, he told this story more than a few times), I always saw his eyes gleaming with emotion, remembering each and every word. From what I can recall from those numerous conversations with my father, his speech to the general went something like this:

"Being the son of a family who did not hesitate to sacrifice their homes, wealth, and safety for the good of this country, today I sit here with great sorrow to tell you I cannot move into my own house. In 1947, my parents migrated from India with pennies in their pockets and a great desire to do something good for this country. Then after many more years of struggle and great sacrifices, they were able to raise a son, myself, who toiled day and night to be a good citizen and get an education so that one day he could live a dignified life. And when the time came that he was able to put a nice roof over his children's heads, his family's sacrifices were forgotten by the government they were made for in the first place. This very same government has become a road block, barring him from moving into his own home. This same government is depriving this citizen of the basic rights of home ownership, and today I sit here in front of you to demand justice for myself, my parents, and my children."

My father then handed the piece of paper to the general, his heart thumping in his throat. Zia-ul-Haq looked my father in the eye and picked up a pen. He signed the order for the premises to be vacated and possession to be delivered to its rightful owner, Mr. Mubashar, effective immediately.

It was a phenomenal triumph to say the least. My father had purchased the house at a huge discount thanks to the stubborn tenant, and as soon as the tenant moved out, the value would skyrocket. He could have made a hefty profit had he decided to sell it, but he's never done that to this day. Had the general dismissed my father that day without doing anything, I might not have spent my childhood in that house. Those memories would not exist.

Unbelievably, even with a signed order from the highest authority in Pakistan, there was still last minute resistance from the tenant, and it took several months to get him out. My father had to threaten going back to General Zia-ul-Haq to complain that his order had not been fulfilled before the tenant finally vacated the premises.

We moved into the house in April of 1986, and I grew up within its walls, living there from age nine to twenty-one, when I moved to the US. This is one of the many reasons why the kidnappers' attempts to steal away its ownership cut deep.

CHAPTER 11
GROWING UP IN PAKISTAN

I was born on February 10, 1977 in a fairly large government hospital situated right in the heart of Islamabad called the Poly Clinic. My father was a government employee, so the care provided there was completely free for our family, which was fortunate because, at the time of my birth, things were kind of "hand to mouth" for my parents. As the family fable goes, at birth, I was stick thin, frail, all wrinkled up, and weighed only five pounds and a few ounces. The nurse who coaxed out my first cry held me up in front of her face and said, "Welcome to this world, old man!"

I would not breastfeed and had severe diarrhea, so the doctor prescribed special, expensive formula milk. This and several other unforeseen expenses that came with the birth of a child (if you are a first time parent, you know what I mean) put a heavy burden on my newlywed parent's finances. My parents needed a way to increase their income, and my mother started looking for a job soon after my birth. It didn't help that my father was financially supporting his mother at the time. My parents lived in government housing my father had obtained through his government service. It was a tiny townhouse located in sector F-6, right in front of a major supermarket literally named the Super Market. The townhouse consisted of two beds, one bath, a living and dining area, a small backyard, and a fair-sized front yard. My father worked at the Manpower Institute in Islamabad for several years and rose to the rank of a Deputy Director. Reaching this status was already a great achievement for my father since he grew up poor in a tiny town near *Chiniot* called *Rabwah*. My father's first childhood memories are set in a world of extreme poverty. His father was chronically ill, and his mother had to work to make ends meet.[7] My father was the third born of four brothers, and as he puts it, out of all his siblings, he was the only one who had any inclination of how to get ahead in life. My father started working as a child, and throughout his life, he had to provide not only for himself, but for his family also. His childhood was full of hardships and hard labor to make ends meet.

My father first moved to Islamabad in 1972 after his graduation and accepted the government job. He rose through the ranks quickly, but his Deputy Director title did not leave him contented. He would continue to work toward establishing his own successful business.

I have a few vague memories of going to the Super Market with my mother when I was three or four years old. My parents also took me to Karachi before my brother and sister were born, so I must have been younger than five, but I still remember it. Back when I was the only child, I lived with my mother in various towns as she traveled across the country for different jobs. Islamabad is a big city with a competitive landscape, and finding a job is not easy. Since both my parents needed to work to cover family expenses, my mother needed to find a job even if it meant she had to go live apart from my father. My mother had an M.A. in Urdu, and there was demand for her

---

[7] I never met with my grandfather. He died before my father's marriage.

skill set, but not so much in Islamabad at the time. When she found one, it was always in a distant city. She took me along with her as she moved from place to place, such as *Bhalwal* and *Mandi Bahauddin*, which are both about two and a half hours' drive away from Islamabad.[8]

I developed a special bond with my mother during those years spent together. However, she was always looking for something in Islamabad so that she could live with her husband, but she had no luck. After a few years of struggle, the closest employment she got was in the town of *Murree*, about two hours away via public transportation, which was the only option she had. While working there, she and I were able to live with my father again, but this meant a daily commute of almost four hours, not to mention a full working day at the college there, teaching Urdu. I was a little over five years old by then, and soon, my brother Ijaz was born. After Ijaz came along, it became more important than ever for my mother to find a local job. As luck would have it, she found employment as an assistant Urdu literature professor at the Government Post Graduate College for Women in the city of *Rawalpindi*, only thirty minutes away.

Growing Up in Islamabad

I lived in that small government townhouse until age ten. In 1986, thanks to my father's successful business dealings, which I have already talked about in chapter 10, we moved to the much bigger house in sector F-7 from which my father was kidnapped. I remember walking to the Super Market either alone or with my parents to buy groceries

---

[8] Nowadays you can do Google search to find these cities on Google Maps

or other household items. It was also a place where people went just for fun and window shopping. From first to fifth grade, I went to a public school in sector F-6 on the opposite side of the Super Market. You might get the kick out of the name, but it was called the Islamabad College for Girls. You might ask why I went to a school that was meant to be for girls only. You see, due to the extreme conservativeness of the country, boys and girls begin to study separately after fifth grade. That's why I moved to the Islamabad Model College for Boys in sector F-7/3 after fifth grade.

My mother (circled) in a ceremony at Rawalpindi's Government Post Graduate College for Women (Undated photo—most likely 1996–97, Source: Author's family albums)

My mother worked at the college in Rawalpindi until her sudden passing on April 04, 1999, due to a brain hemorrhage at the age of fifty-three. My father never remarried or showed any interest in it.

The struggles my parent's endured in the early years of their marriage fueled my father to leave his government job, start his own company, and become a very successful businessman.

The making of a shining star

By the time we moved into the house my father was kidnapped from, I had already transferred to the Islamabad Model College for Boys, located in sector F-7/3, nearer to my home. I must admit that I was an average student up until seventh grade. A typical class in Pakistan has about thirty pupils, and in those days, you did not get letter grades in exams but "marks" instead, such as 100/100 or 50/100. Then these marks would be combined from various subjects, such as English, Urdu, Mathematics, etc., and a total was created. The pupil who had the most marks would be ranked as top of the class, the pupil who had second highest marks would get second position, and so on and so forth.

This harsh grading and ranking system starts in Pakistan from grade one. At the end of every exam, pupils are given report cards with their total marks, and they are told who is first in class, who is last, and who is a complete failure. In my class of thirty, I was always around seventh or eighth—occasionally fifth position if I was lucky and the top student fell sick during exams, and even tenth or twelfth at times. The students that secured the top three positions were considered the brightest students, and it was open secret shared with every student and all the parents.

My bad buddy and flunking an exam

You always have turning points in your life that you remember in vivid detail, moments that cause you to change direction briskly, for the better in most cases. This moment came to me in sixth grade. In those days, I fell into the wrong company, hanging out with students who did not do well in their exams and who were always finding someone to help them cheat. The classrooms were small, and the students were crammed side by side. However, if you wanted to cheat by reading off someone else's paper, you had to get that person to agree to allow you to do so, or you risked the other student noticing and complaining to the teacher. One of my new buddies told me just before one math exam that his friend, the ring leader of their little gang, was not prepared. My friend told me this boy would sit right next to me, and I must allow him to copy all the answers from my worksheet. I don't know what I was thinking, but I agreed. This math exam was an important one that led up to the finals.

Incidentally, our math teacher, Sir Yusuf, knew my mother. As a result, he tried to pay special attention to me even though I was definitely not the star student of his class. Come the exam day, I allowed my newfound buddy to sit right next to me so he could copy my answers. Typically, Sir Yusuf was seen as a poor monitor, as he often read his newspaper during the test, paying little attention to what students were doing. This lax behavior might have been a factor in why I agreed to let my buddy copy my exam. When the exam began, I started filling out my sheets, and my "friend" was in hot pursuit. The thing was, I was ill prepared for the exam myself because hanging out with the wrong company had allowed me to study little. I was also quite nervous about allowing someone to copy from me, and this nervousness slowed me down in this timed exam; I was well aware that I could be kicked out of school for doing this. Even worse, my bad buddy turned out to be a very slow copycat. When I finished a sheet of paper, he wouldn't let me turn over to the next until he had finished copying.

Needless to say, I was not able to finish the exam that day; I didn't even get halfway. As much as Sir Yusuf was enjoying his newspaper, the moment time was up, he threw it aside and started to collect back the exam sheets. If I remember correctly, I made a plea to allow a few more minutes, which fell on deaf ears. I knew I was in trouble. I had already started to resent my buddy and complained to him about how slow he'd worked. To my amazement, he couldn't care less. Failing an exam was not an issue for him, but it was not acceptable to me in any way. Sure enough, when the exam results came back in about one week, I found out I had flunked. Sir Yusuf looked astonished when he handed over my report card.

"What went wrong, Syed?" he asked me more than once. "Were you perhaps feeling sick during the exam?" I did not have an answer for him, and I just stood there like a statue.

School photo with famous cricketer Imran Khan as chief guest, circled upfront (sitting in the middle). Your author can be seen circled standing in the back (no glasses). My copycat buddy is also circled in front of me (with glasses). Imran Khan has since made a name for himself in Pakistani politics. (Date: 1987, Source: Author's family albums)

My mother's plea, and the making of an "A" student

I knew I was in grave trouble. My parents placed the highest emphasis on education, and they had made it clear to me that they were willing to honor all my wishes if I brought home good grades. I was not allowed to go out and play with friends, watch a movie, etc. unless I finished my homework first. During exam weeks, all extracurricular activities would come to a complete halt so that I could prepare. There were rewards tied to good performances in the exams, but allowances were also withheld for subpar performances. This horrendous math grade wreaked havoc at home, just as I'd suspected it would.

Although I did not tell Sir Yusuf the real reason for my failure, I broke down in front of my mother when she asked me. I felt I had to tell her the truth, that my cheating assistance had caused me not to finish my exam in the allotted time. My mother was flabbergasted. She actually burst into tears. I knew if my father found out, he would do something, but it probably wouldn't be cry. However, my father never talked to me about the incident, and I do not know to this day if he ever knew about this failure. If my mother told him, it was with the condition that he would spare me this time.

My mother arranged an emergency meeting with Sir Yusuf. In the meeting, Sir Yusuf told my mother he had felt something was wrong and that I was trying to hide something, but he could not quite put his finger on it. I recall badly wanting to say, "I really wish you hadn't been reading that newspaper."

I remember Sir Yusuf quite clearly. He wore thick glasses and had a French-cut, salt and pepper beard. The backside of his head was balding, leaving only a little hair around his forehead. He had the demeanor of an evil scientist, and he used to forget his own questions right after asking them. Since the day he'd handed me back that failed test, he must have asked me why I had failed the exam ten times. My first thought was that I should just lie and make an excuse that I was sick that day and thus ill prepared for the exam. But since I had told my mother the truth, and she was sitting right next to me in the meeting, I had to tell the truth. Sir Yusuf stared at me in disbelief, but there was something in his eyes that belied mixed feelings of anger and pity. I think the teacher-to-teacher respect between my mother and Sir Yusuf is to thank for his soft treatment of me that day. He could have reported me to school authorities and had me expelled. I do not know to this day what kind of action Sir Yusuf took against my buddy, though he was not kicked out of school, but he let me go with a warning to never try anything remotely similar again. My mother ordered me to call it quits with my new copycat friend and anyone else in his group for that matter, and I did. When we got home, my mother looked at me with deep sadness in her eyes and said, "I make sure my master level students pass with flying colors, and here is my own son failing an exam in sixth grade math. This is a very low point in my life!"

It was fair to say that it was also a low point in my life. To let my mother down was something I did not take lightly. My mother's emotional outburst and deep disappointment in me had a profound effect that would change me forever. From that very day, I made a firm decision to get serious and prove to my parents, especially my mother, that I was capable of becoming an exceptional student.

From that point onward, I decided to become a much more focused student. I became fast friends with the number one student in our class, Usman Malik.⁹ He actually became my best friend as time went on. I always sat beside him in class to cut back on distraction. I went to his house in the evenings to find out how he studied and how he completed his homework. He was glad to help. I remember after about a year, it was well known in school that we were best buddies. Our friendship extended outside school, too. I used to ride my bicycle to his house in the evenings to study or play with him. However, I can barely recall a single instance when he visited me at my home, but I was okay with that.

After becoming best friends with Usman, who had been number one consistently for the last two years, and spending about four/five months in his company, I started to see major improvements in my academic career. Studying was becoming more fun; at least, I no longer hated it. I was able to memorize things more easily by making up games and strategies in my head. I became highly disciplined in my daily activities, creating a strict schedule for when I was supposed to do homework and when I had time to play. I followed this schedule so rigidly that, in one instance, my mother had to laugh at me because she saw me timing myself eating a meal.

The next exam was fast approaching, and I was studying hard, knowing that I was under the scrutiny of my parents. When exams started, my mother actually had to go out of town for work, but she told me she had complete faith in me before she left. When the final results came in two weeks later, I was in fourth position. Not a bad feat, rising from eighth to fourth within six months. Both my mother and Sir Yusuf were extremely pleased.

I still have that report card tucked away somewhere at home.

I was ecstatic about the results, but the most important thing for

---

[9] There were actually three students by the name of Usman in my class.

me was that I had made my mother happy in the process. I decided that I was not going to stop there. I kept studying ever harder with Usman. Not only did I learn from his study techniques, but I actually built upon them. As Sir Isaac Newton once said, "If I have seen farther than others, it is by standing upon the shoulders of giants."

If Usman told me that he had studied for three hours that day, I would try to beat him and study for four. I continued working hard, and it was showing. The homework and class projects I was producing and my keen interest to do more than was asked for was pleasantly surprising many teachers. Many other students were coming to me for help, which I gladly provided. I was just genuinely interested in studying. I often tried to study ahead myself at home. In just under a year, I had transformed into a completely new student.

Biology exam and surprising my teacher

During midterm week, one of our biology teachers, Sir Sami, gave the class a regular lecture in the period right before the exam was to be administered, quickly going through a new chapter on human evolution. He specifically asked us to listen carefully to his lecture that day. His statement struck me as odd and made me pay attention. Shouldn't he be expecting students to listen carefully every day of the week?

The basic rule of midterm exams was that the material must be chosen from previously covered chapters and not a chapter taught the same day. This was done to avoid being unfair since students would be unable to prepare for the material ahead of time.

However, Sir Sami was about to break this rule. After the bell rang for the next period, he announced that the test would be just two multiple-choice questions—one from a prior chapter and the other from the human evolution chapter he'd just taught. The problem was that many students had completely tuned out during the lecture, never thinking that the material might appear on the exam, even after Sir Sami had warned us to pay special attention. Luckily, I had taken his comment seriously and listened carefully as he talked about how life forms first originated on the earth's surface and how, due to temperatures becoming more moderate, amoebas and single-celled organisms became more and more complex until animals and then eventually human beings were formed. To tell you the truth, I had studied this chapter ahead of time at home because I was genuinely interested in the topic.

However, most of my fellow students yawned at it, rehearsing older material in their heads in preparation for the exam during this lecture. Students were known to hide exam subject books underneath their present class subject books to study during normal class hours for the upcoming exam. I could tell by their stunned faces that the students around me hadn't been paying any attention.

Sir Sami told us that we only had to attempt one question, and I decided without hesitation that I would attempt the question on human evolution. As I wrote out my answer, I felt some nervousness, but I also felt the excitement of attempting something still fresh in my mind. The results were announced a week later.

When Sir Sami came into the classroom the day of the grade announcement, he gave a short lecture on the importance of listening skills inside the classroom. Then he surprised the whole class by pointing at me and saying that I was the only person in the whole class who even attempted the question on human evolution. He then said something I will never forget.

"In my mind, all of you have flunked this exam, even if not literally," he said. "Only this guy"—he jabbed his finger at me again—"has actually passed this exam."

I felt honored. I had obtained the highest marks, 24/25, by attempting this question. Like rest of the class, Usman had chosen the question on prior material and got 23/25, which was the second highest score. When Sir Sami returned my exam sheet, I saw there were numerous errors in my essay, and when I compared my essay to that of Usman, he actually had fewer errors. I realized I was given extra credit for being bold and taking on Sir Sami's challenge.

Time flew and eight months later, I ranked third in the whole class in our semifinals. In just two years, I had moved up from flunking to having the third highest grade. My parents and all my teachers were extremely happy with my progress, but not everyone felt the same. Usman started to act strange. I started to feel some resentment from him whenever I got special attention or praise from the teachers. I had felt it burn especially strong when Sir Sami put me in the spotlight, usually reserved for Usman, after that biology test. But he continued to sit next to me and hang out with me after school. He was still the number one student in the class and may have thought that this attention to me would be short lived. During those times, no one was even trying to compete for the number one spot. It was reserved for Usman. Everyone was competing for second or third. He was just untouchable.

Still, I noticed a shift in his demeanor toward me. He used to go out of his way to help me study and complete assignments, but now he was not as keen to help as before. I did not always need as much help anymore anyway, but nevertheless, being an open-minded person, I was always willing to learn something from the top student. However, it so happened that he was getting opportunities to learn a thing or two from me as well. Instead of receiving all the value in the friendship, I was able to bring a lot of value to him also. Despite his new, somewhat aloof attitude toward me, I still sat right next to him in class and kept up the friendship.

The eighth grade year was coming to an end, and finals were fast approaching. I was working harder than ever, studying like a mad man. I was aiming for second position, figuring that was the next logical jump. This goal seemed more realistic than ever, although it would have seemed like a pipe dream only a couple of years before. I had developed quite intensive study techniques and had learned ways to absorb a lot more material in a very short period of time.

My mother was the greatest support for me during that time. Not only was she extremely pleased with my progress, but she was also a constant source of encouragement, pushing me to do better and better. She was absolutely ecstatic about the complete change of heart I'd undergone when it came to academics. Only a couple of years before, my mother would be called into the school to be told, "Your son is a failure," but now she was called in and told, "Your son is doing great." I think she must have liked that feeling.

Who will break the previous school record?

When finals week arrived, I was prepared, and it all went by in a flash. I felt great about my performance, but the results would not be announced for the next couple of weeks.

In our school, final results were announced in the auditorium in a big ceremony in which a "chief guest" would be invited, along with all the parents. After the chief guest finished with his opening remarks, our school principal would walk to the podium and announce the top three students in each grade, starting from the first grade and ending with the tenth grade.

The ceremony started with big fanfare. The chief guest (whom I don't seem to recall) made an opening speech and the principal congratulated those who would be promoted to the next grade. Excited parents and relatives were crammed into the auditorium along with the students, and as the principal began announcing who was third, second, and first in the first grade, the roar of clapping and cheering began. Each named student would walk up onstage to receive their prize—Legos, a book, a pencil box, or some other small school supply item. When the first place student in seventh grade was announced, my heart was in my mouth; my grade was next. Third place went to Usman Hassan (not to be confused with my best study pal, Usman Malik), who was also a good friend of mine.[10]

Usman Hassan went up onstage, received his prize from the principal, and came back down with a big smile on his face. Second position was next, and I wanted it so bad my heart was pounding at supersonic speeds.

"God, please let this be me, please let this be me," I prayed in my head.

This was my only chance; everyone knew who was going to be first, and it wasn't me. If the principal didn't say my name, it meant

---

[10] When I was in Islamabad in 2016, I got together with Usman Hassan, and we went hiking together on Margalla Hills. We'd taken that same hike once in school, so it jogged up some good memories.

I was in fourth or fifth position or, God forbid, back in seventh and eighth. I didn't think I could handle that.

"Second position is secured by Usman Malik!"

"Usman Malik?" The whispered question spread throughout the gathered eighth grade students. It ought to be a mistake. Usman had to be first, right? He'd been first in everything since the sixth grade. As Usman rose from his seat to collect his prize, I saw the bland, unsmiling expression on his face. My fellow classmates and I exchanged puzzled looks. The same question was written on everyone's face. If Usman Malik wasn't first, who was?

Frankly, I had lost all hope for myself. I knew if I was not second, as I'd hoped, then I was probably fourth or fifth. Anything lower would really break my heart. My third place win at midterms didn't seem so great now. I figured I had just been lucky, that maybe the other students hadn't studied hard enough. Then again, I was at a loss to come up with a name for who could be first apart from Usman. So I was alert, waiting with anticipation like all the others, as I watched Usman come down from the stage with his prize firmly tucked in his hands and a light smile on his face this time.

As Usman sat down, the principal looked again at his list of names. Time froze, and a daring thought flashed through my mind.

What if I was the top student?

I shrugged off the thought as soon as it came. It had to be Zeeshan, I assured myself. He was bright, and he routinely came in second or third on tests. Quite frankly, I was just hoping that when we all went back to our classrooms and checked the full lists, I would be fourth.

Then the principal's voice echoed through the hall. "First position is secured by Syed Saqib!"

Surely I was dreaming. I pinched my arm to make sure. From both sides of my chair, my classmates were looking at me with amazement. Those awed and smiling faces gave me some assurance that my ears were not ringing and that my name was indeed just called. It took me couple of seconds to gain my composure and get up from my seat. The principal, who was also our English teacher, greeted me with a broad smile, congratulated me, and handed over my prize and report card. When I returned to my seat, my classmates were giggling at my expression and congratulating me. Once I was seated, I looked at my report card, just to confirm it was all true. To say I was ecstatic would be the understatement of the century.

The principal continued his announcements for ninth and tenth grade, and that meant it was time to announce the top student in the entire school for the year. This would be the person who, in any grade, had secured the most marks and obtained the highest percentage in all his finals. I was so absorbed in looking at my prize and report card and joking around with my friends that I was not even paying attention.

"The top student of the year award goes to Syed Saqib!"

My head shot up when I heard my name. This was some kind of a cruel dream; it would all be gone when I woke up. It hadn't really been my name, had it? My feet felt heavy and glued to the ground. I did not budge from my seat. What if I was hallucinating? What if I had heard wrong, and I got up just to be told to sit down again? The whole crowd would roar with laughter. I could almost hear a phantom voice taunting me, "Sit down, smarty pants. It's not you."

I was looking for some affirmation that I was not being delusional. Finally, a gentle elbow nudge from my classmate next to me broke my trance.

"Syed, get up, man. He called your name!"

As I rose from my seat, I quickly glanced around to make sure that there was no other Syed Saqib rising from his seat also in the hall. No one else moved, and the growing sound of clapping in the hall enhanced my confidence some more, so I kept walking toward the stage. Once I was up there, the principal greeted me again with a big smile, shook my hand, and handed me the award for being the highest-scoring student for the year of 1988. Not only was I the highest-scoring student of the year, I had actually broken the prior record by securing an aggregate ninety-six percent. [11]

A photo of me receiving the student of the year award from Principal Rafique Malik. (Date: 1988, Source: Author's family albums)

Not everything about this story was happy. Those of you who have attained any level of success in life probably know that once you begin to surpass other people, you are often the subject of jealousy

---

[11] Unfortunately, both my mother and father could not make it to this ceremony that day, for reasons I cannot recall, which I would regret for the rest of my life.

and resentment from others. The harsh lesson I learned from that milestone experience was that this jealousy could even fester in the hearts of those you once called your best friends. That is exactly what happened between Usman and me. Right after I became the top student in class, he ended his friendship with me. He stopped sitting next to me in the classroom. He stopped studying with me. He stopped inviting me over. We were soon not even on speaking terms. Our rivalry became the talk of the school.

The loss of his friendship was a blow, but I didn't let it slow me down. I remained the top student until tenth grade when I left for another institution, helping as many other students as possible whenever I could along the way.

Matriculation Exams and being at the top again

As I finished up tenth grade in 1992, the Intermediate Board Exams loomed over my head at the end of the year. Pakistan's education system gives this exam extreme importance because it dictates your career path. Once you are in eleventh grade, you have to choose your profession, and you are assigned coursework based on your choice. Thus, students have to start thinking about which college they want to get into in tenth grade.[12] You want to find the best school with the best programs for your career path. The only way you can get into a prestigious school is to get good marks on the Federal Board Exam.

The Matriculation Exam is also referred to as the Federal Board Exam because the Federal Board oversees all private and public

---
[12] In Pakistan, eleventh and twelfth grade are called "college," and after that you go to "university" to obtain your professional degree.

schools in Islamabad, and this is their system-wide exam. The idea is to test students with common material to gage their overall skill set. There is a total of eight hundred and fifty marks on the exam, and the student who obtains the highest marks is said to have "topped" the Federal Board.

I am proud to say that I placed third in all of the Federal Board Exams taken in 1992, out of about twenty thousand students. I secured a total of 750/850. My name is still engraved on the Honor Board of Islamabad Model College for Boys in F-7/3, Islamabad. When I visited Pakistan with my family in 2011, I actually took my wife and then two-year-old son to my alma mater, and we took pictures in front of that Honor Board. Due to my high placement, a couple of prominent newspapers in Islamabad wrote about me.

Newspaper cuttings announcing my third place placement in the Federal Board Exams. (Date: June 1992, Source: Author's family albums)

Because I was among the top performers in the Federal Board Exams, I was accepted at a top notch college in Pakistan in a pre-engineering program. The name of this institution is "Cadet College,

Hasan Abdal", located in town called Hasan Abdal, which is about two hours' drive away from Islamabad. There are a couple of unique things about this college:

1. You must live in a hostel at the college
2. No matter how many marks you have obtained in Federal Board Exam, you have to pass their own entry test

Thus, I took the entry test for Cadet College Hasan Abdal in 1992, passed it and got admitted in this college. I stayed in this college from 1992 to 1994 from grades 11 to 12. Then at the end of grade 12, there is another very important exam called "Faculty of Science (FSC) Board Exam", which qualifies you to actually being admitted to different universities in various disciplines such as engineering, medical, finance, etc. I again toiled over my studies, and when the Board Exams were finished, I was once again among the top students in the whole board, comprised of about thirty thousand students in 1994. I placed fourth in the whole of the Rawalpindi Board, the jurisdiction in which Cadet College belongs. I secured a total of 951/1,100. Again, some prominent newspapers in Pakistan, such as the *Pakistan Times*, wrote stories about me, one of which you can find below. It was a big honor for my family and me.

Newspaper cuttings of the article written about me because of my high performance in the Board Exam. (Date: September 1994, Source: Author's family albums)

Six years after I'd surprised myself by being the top student in my school in Islamabad, I was a part of another award ceremony, this time at Cadet College, Hasan Abdal, where I was awarded a prize and a medal of honor. This time there were no surprises. The most important thing about this ceremony was that both of my parents were present, cheering for me from the crowd.

A photo of me receiving a prize for securing the overall fourth position in all of the Rawalpindi Board at Cadet College, Hasan Abdal. (Date: November 16, 1994, Source: Author's family albums)

Afterward, I was admitted into the most elite engineering university in Pakistan, the National University of Sciences and Technology (NUST), and finished my degree in electrical engineering from there in about three years with honors. After finishing my degree, I came to the US in August 1998 and completed my master's in electrical engineering in June of 2000. Since then, I have held various positions and have moved around to many places within the United States, such as Nashville, Tennessee (from 2000 to 2003), Dallas, Texas (from 2003 to 2005), Phoenix, Arizona (2005-2006), St. Louis, Missouri (2005 to 2007), and finally Chicago, Illinois, where I have been since 2007. I also completed an MBA in finance in 2011 from DePaul University in Chicago. As of this writing, I am happily settled in Chicago with my wife and two sons, ages four and seven.

CHAPTER 12

MY RIDE ALONG WITH POLICE

I remained heavily involved with the police and Mr. Iqbal from February 25–28, 2016, before my father was discharged from the hospital on February 28. My father's last two days were relatively quiet, and he was resting a lot. As a matter of fact, the hospital had told us as early as February 25 that he was good to go home, but it was upon our insistence he was allowed to stay for few more days.

Bank visits with police

In the meantime, I worked with the Kohsar senior inspector assigned to the case. We went to the two banks that were looted by Sadaf, the female accomplice, using my father's checks: Standard Chartered Bank in the Super Market (one of the big shopping centers in Islamabad) and Dubai Bank in F-10/3 Markaz (another huge shopping center). The irony was that Dubai Bank was renting space owned by my father.

We went to Standard Chartered Bank first, on February 26, with a constable in tow.

When we reached the bank, an attractive receptionist, who asked us who we were looking for, greeted us. She eyed the two police officers nervously, knowing something was wrong. She ushered us upstairs to the manager's office and asked us to have a seat while we waited. Though it was a busy morning in the bank, the manager showed up before too long and greeted everyone graciously before asking the purpose of our visit. The inspector told the manager that someone had withdrawn a total of Rs. 1,900,000 (roughly $19,000 US) from Mr. Mubashar's account and that police would like information about that person. The inspector asked for details of all withdrawals made between February 10 and February 16 and asked about the banks' withdraw procedure for large sums.

The bank manager explained that the procedure was threefold. First, the owner of the account is called. (They had followed this step; not knowing my father was being held at gunpoint when he gave consent.) Second, the bank obtains a copy of the person's National Identity Card (NIC) withdrawing funds, which is issued by the Government of Pakistan to every citizen. Lastly, a video recording automatically captures anyone at the counter interacting with cashiers.

The inspector asked for a copy of the NIC and video footage of the person who had made the transaction from my father's account, and the manager readily complied without even asking for a court order. I think police presence was enough to convince him that fraud had taken place at his bank. Since the transaction was only a couple of weeks old, the manager located the photocopies of the NIC without any trouble. This was how we first learned the identity of Sadaf Hassan Raza.

Unfortunately, the live footage of Raza wouldn't be available for two weeks, because it had to be ordered from another location. We took manager's contact information and told him that we would check back in a couple of weeks.

After leaving Standard Chartered Bank, we made the twenty-minute drive to Dubai Bank in F-10 Markaz. The staff there was equally puzzled by the presence of two police officers. The manager there was a relatively young man who asked us to sit down and offered us green tea, which was incidentally the best green tea I have ever had, with subtle hints of lemon and sweetness that was ambrosial on the tongue. Seriously, it was good. As I sat sipping it, a smile came over my face; it was pretty fun traveling with these police officers.

The same requests were made to this manager. The NIC, once again handed over without a court order, showed the same exact woman, Sadaf Hassan Raza (privacy laws in Pakistan are not that strict, and simple police presence probably made this request legitimate). She stole Rs. 900,000 (about $9,000 US) from this bank. The Dubai manager told us that obtaining the footage could take up to ten days.

It was about 1:00 p.m. when we finished up, and I knew the officers expected me to treat them to lunch. This is how things typically work in Pakistan, especially with police. Even though they were doing their appointed duty, they still expected to be pampered. Well, actually, they were not even doing their job, since I was the one hauling them around in my personal vehicle. No police vehicle had been available that day, according to them. Had I requested the use of a police vehicle, I can guarantee you all their excuses would have delayed the process by several days.

Still, I knew if I did not treat them to lunch, they might feel like they weren't being taken care of in the manner they thought they rightfully (or wrongfully) deserved, and they might create more obstacles for me down the road. Upsetting them in anyway was the last thing I wanted to do. So off we went to a restaurant, where they proceeded to order the most expensive items on the menu.

CHAPTER 13

THE NORWEGIAN NARCOTICS CHIEF

While still in the hospital, my father gave me the contact number of a potential renter who was trying to lease the back portion of his house. His name was Khalid, and my father had met with him several times before the kidnapping. If you remember, the back portion of the home is like a second full residence, with four bedrooms, three bathrooms, and its own garage.

Khalid was a Norwegian national who was sent to Pakistan by the Government of Norway to work under the umbrella of the Norwegian Consulate in Islamabad. He and my father had already drafted a rough contract (referred to as an agreement in Pakistan). They had been well on their way to finalizing the details, such as who would pay for electricity, gas, maintenance, etc., before my father was kidnapped. The agreement was supposed to be sent to the Norwegian Consulate for final approval, but my father had been "missing" for the better part of a month now. As soon as he had recovered somewhat, the first thing on his mind was getting in touch with Khalid and keeping him engaged, and he gave the task to me.

However, he instructed me not to mention anything about kidnapping and just tell Khalid that he was recovering in the hospital from an illness.

If memory serves me correctly, I called Khalid either on the 23rd or the 24th. I introduced myself as Mubashar's son and informed him that I would like to meet with him regarding their lease negotiations. I also told him that my father was recovering from an illness in the hospital and that he would be back home soon to finalize the last few details of the agreement. We agreed on a time to meet briefly at the house the next day so that I could update him on my father's condition and have a chance to meet him in person.

According to my father, they had agreed upon a rate of Rs. 500,000 ($5,000 US) per month. One year's worth of rent, Rs. 6,000,000 ($60,000 US) was to be paid up front at the time of the signing. This was a large sum by any calculation, and my father was more than mildly interested in getting the lease in place as soon as possible. If you live outside Pakistan, a seller asking for a full year's rent in advance and a buyer easily agreeing to such a term is undoubtedly strange.

Expecting advance rent in upscale neighborhoods is commonplace in Pakistan, especially in overheated rental markets. As a successful realtor and broker, my father has facilitated hundreds of transactions in which he was successfully able to get not only one year's advance rent but sometimes even two. Before the tragedy that occurred on September 11, 2001, Pakistan was seen as a safe country with strict law and order. As the capital city, Islamabad, with all its foreign missions and embassies, was the safest place of all. Since any country with diplomatic relations with Pakistan must establish a presence via a consulate or embassy in the capital, the Pakistani government has dedicated a full sector in Islamabad, dubbed F-5 or the Diplomatic Enclave, exclusively to foreign missions.

Back in the 1980s and 1990s, when things used to be relatively stable in Pakistan, the foreign employees working for the embassies had two choices:

1. Live in the residences available within the Diplomatic Enclave. Typically, these would be small apartments as opposed to a house.

2. Seek accommodations outside the Diplomatic Enclave in neighboring sectors, which would not only be larger, but also cheaper in many cases.

Now imagine you are a high-ranking employee of a consulate who has come to Pakistan with his family, looking for a place to live. Would you rather live in a tiny apartment within the embassy compound, or would you want to live in a full-fledged house no more than thirty minutes away in another sector? Keep in mind that rent on the house might come out slightly cheaper than the apartment. Furthermore, by living outside the Diplomatic Enclave, which is just a business district, you would have readier access to shopping and other fun activities.

Needless to say, many foreigners chose to live outside sector F-5, and the closest surrounding sectors became the natural choices for foreigners. Thus sectors F6–F7–F8, situated around the foothills of a scenic mountain range called Margalla Hills, became "hot neighborhoods."

Since these sectors were in high demand from locals as well as the foreign employees, rents and mortgages went through the roof in the mid-1980s and held steady throughout the 1990s and early

2000s. With rents skyrocketing, landlords started to impose other demands to whittle down the number of potential tenants in an overheated market, one of which was requiring multiple months' rent in advance. When tenants complied without complaint and the market showed no signs of slowing down, landlords started to demand years' worth of rent in advance just because they could.

I saw this all firsthand, as I used to draft lease agreements (sometimes with up to three years' advanced payment included) for my father on his old office computer (a rare possession back then) during his real estate hey-days in the 1990s, when he generated most of his wealth.

Hot real estate market or just a bubble?

Now you may ask, "Who could possibly afford to pay a full two to three years' worth of rent upfront?" Well, foreign employees were not paying out of pocket; their governments paid on their behalf. Thus, all an employee needed to do was apprise his or her government of the norms of Islamabad's rental market, and more often than not, the government would issue the whopping checks to landlords without too many questions.

Wealthy locals as well as embassy employees were attempting to lease space in these desirable sectors, so property values also went through the roof. This allowed the landlords to demand triple net (NNN) leases on residential property. A triple net lease simply means that the tenant is responsible for all property maintenance, insurance, and taxes. The landlord is responsible for nothing, zilch, nada! All the landlords had to do was show up at the end of two years and collect another two years' worth of rent, should the tenant agree to renew the lease, and trust me, many of them did. This is unheard of in many parts of the world, especially Western countries where triple net leases only exist in commercial real estate (and that is only in hot markets such as New York, San Francisco, etc.), not residential. I have lived in the US since 1998 and have never come across a residential landlord who would dare demand a triple net lease from a tenant.

Due to this property craze, the value of my father's properties increased rapidly also. These skyrocketing property values are one big reason why my father has done so well in a country like Pakistan, where an ordinary citizen still lives on less than $2,000 per year. My father bought his current residence in 1985 for Rs. 600,000 which is approximately $36,000 with inflation. If my father were to sell this house today, he could easily fetch Rs. 120,000,000 (about $1.2 million, given the 2016 exchange rate). That's an increase of about 33 times in thirty years, which is 12.36% return compounded annually where the average rate of increase in residential property value in the developed world remains at 4-5% annually. Not too shabby for a real estate investment, wouldn't you agree?

Then came the terrorist attacks of September 11, 2001, which affected Pakistan more than most people realize. The United States went to war with neighboring Afghanistan, which indirectly created many problems for Pakistan. The country became buried in a myriad of issues due to the influx of insurgents escaping Afghanistan, which rapidly deteriorated the security landscape, not to mention the fact that these unwanted individuals later became part of al-Qaeda and formed bases in Pakistan.

As security and law and order deteriorated, Pakistan was viewed as an unsafe country, which probably stands true even today. Slowly and steadily, foreign missions started to reduce staff in Pakistan. Those officials who had brought their whole families were now sending them back home. Their governments then started questioning them about the big houses they were living in and whether such accommodation was really necessary. When the leases came due, the governments asked their employees to move inside the Diplomatic Enclave and get a smaller apartment fit for a single person. Not only would it save cost, the Diplomatic Enclave is considered to be a much safer area because the Pakistani government itself is in charge of security for foreign missions. There is a gated entrance, and you cannot enter the sector without going through security. Hence, there was a major exodus from the surrounding sectors in the years following 2001.

Now the same landlords who had demanded two years' worth of advanced rent relaxed their requirements to one year, or six months in some cases. The property values started to collapse and continued to rapidly decline from 2004 to 2014, only slowing in recent years. My father felt the effects of the collapse, too. As an example, he has an investment property in Islamabad that he has owned since 1996, which is leased by a Christian church. He was getting two years' worth of advanced rent until 2010 when the church announced they could only pay one year's worth. When the lease renewal date rolled back around, they asked for six months' worth. By the time I arrived in 2016, my father was only getting three months' rent in advance, and the church was asking for further concessions going forward.

This downturn in real estate value in Islamabad has made many landlords desperate, and my father is no exception. Therefore, when this Norwegian tenant, Khalid, showed up with an offer to pay one year's rent in advance, my father was very excited.

Meeting with the Norwegian renter for the first time

I met Khalid at the front gate of the house. Although not terribly overweight, Khalid was a heavyset gentleman. He had a thick moustache, but the hair on his head was thinning at the top. He appeared to be in his mid-fifties. He spoke English with a heavy European accent that I could not quite place. His Pakistani name made me suspect he had been born there. However, when his cell phone rang during our meeting, he spoke in a language that I assumed was Norwegian. I thought it might not be too polite to ask him about his origins during our first meeting, especially when he was already acquainted with my father. I assumed that my father must have done a background check on him since he had met him several times already and the lease negotiations were underway. I did not want to offend him by asking nagging questions.

We never went inside during that first brief meeting, choosing instead to stand out on the street. I introduced myself and explained that I had just arrived from the US. I told him my father had become ill and was recovering in the hospital. Although he showed concern for my father, he did not ask too many questions. He introduced himself as an employee of the Norwegian government, sent to Pakistan to act as the chief of the narcotics task force. He said that this task force was assigned to stop the illegal flow of drugs from Pakistan into European countries, most importantly Norway. He told me he was not at liberty to divulge any more information, because his task force belonged to a secret arm of Norway's law enforcement.

The Norwegian government had given him enough leeway to get the dwelling of his choice anywhere in Islamabad. According to him, although our available space was on the higher end of his budget ($5,000 per month), he could most likely make it work out so that his government would pay. He had already obtained a verbal approval from his boss in Islamabad and was only awaiting final approval from Norway. Once officially approved, he would receive a check amounting to $60,000 for the first year's worth of rent.

I told him that I would keep him in the loop regarding my father's condition, and as soon as my father was back from the hospital, we would arrange another meeting.

After saying farewell to Khalid, I went to PIMS and told my father that the meeting had gone well and that the potential tenant still wanted to move forward with the lease. I also told him that his hospital stay hadn't raised any red flags with Khalid. My father was relieved; his biggest concern was that if Khalid found out about the kidnapping, it might leave a bad taste in his mouth that would make him rethink his decision to lease. My father asked me to keep him in the loop if Khalid called before his discharge from the hospital.

Sure enough, I received a text from Khalid on February 27 saying that the "big check" had been dispatched from Norway and that he needed to meet my father as soon as possible. However, my father was still in the hospital and not in good enough shape to meet with anyone, let alone finalize the details of a lease agreement. I politely replied to Khalid, saying that he needed to wait another couple of days until my father was discharged, and we could arrange a meeting at our home shortly thereafter. He agreed without any hesitation, and I quickly relayed the good news about the check to my father.

Looking at him lying there in that hospital bed, I was worried that my father would not be in good enough shape to meet with Khalid even after his discharge. I prayed Khalid wouldn't make a big issue about his health and ask too many probing questions about what had happened. If Khalid somehow found out he was moving into a house targeted by kidnappers, and that they might still be watching the residence, I was sure it would all fall apart. There was little I could do except keep my fingers crossed. I was eager for the deal to work out because Khalid appeared polite and agreeable during all communications with him, and I thought he would make an excellent tenant. Whether my gut was right remained to be seen.

CHAPTER 14

WITH FRIENDS LIKE THESE

On February 27, everyone involved in my father's care—the general practitioner, cardiologist, urologist, psychiatrist, and a number of nurses—held a large meeting to discuss his condition. The general consensus was that he was stable enough for discharge.

I took my father home from PIMS around 10 a.m. on February 28, 2016. He was still not feeling too well and was visibly sick. He still had regular urges to go to the bathroom. So much so, there was some reservation on his part about whether he would be able to make the fifteen-minute drive home without accident. He used the bathroom once more just before leaving and then I helped him to the car. Peter sat in the back with him. Fiza and her son rode in the front with me. (Apparently it is not an issue in Pakistan to have a baby unsecured in a mother's lap in the passenger seat. In the US, you would probably have your license revoked for something like that.) As soon as we pulled into traffic, my father needed the bathroom. There was no way out of the long line of cars. Somehow, he managed to make it home. He climbed the stairs to the second floor where his bedroom was and rushed straight to the bathroom. I could not get my head around why he needed to go so often. I asked Fiza her professional opinion on the matter, and she said she would look into it shortly. Dad wanted to go to sleep as soon as he finished in the bathroom, so Fiza and I moved to the neighboring room and started chatting about what our game plan was going to be, keeping an eye on our father as we did. It quickly became apparent he was getting up every few minutes for the bathroom. We heard his shoes clapping on the marble floor each time he made his way down the hall, and he always slammed the door a little too hard. When he got up from his nap in the afternoon, I asked Fiza to take a closer look at him. She gently pressed on his bladder and found it was swollen. However, she was not sure what that meant or how it would affect him. I suggested we call Ali.

As you have doubtless realized by now, Ali hates driving. When I called and asked him to come by to take a look at my father, he said I'd need to pick him up from his house. So I drove right back to the PIMS campus for the second time that day.

Even though Ali is a cardiologist, he has experience as a general practitioner. He is well qualified to perform regular check-ups on patients. After a quick examination, he announced that my father's bladder was full of urine and must be drained with a "Foley" immediately. A Foley catheter (named for its designer, Frederic Foley) is a flexible tube passed through the urethra and into the bladder. A little balloon inflates inside the bladder to keep the tube from slipping out while the urine is drained. The only problem was that Ali hadn't brought one with him. He and I sped to a drug store in the Jinnah supermarket ten minutes away to grab one.

As the Foley emptied my father's bladder, and I could see the instant relief on his face. A later diagnosis revealed that my father's prostate gland was swollen, which was causing him all the discomfort during urination. He had to make constant bathroom trips because his bladder was never completely emptied. We learned later that swelling of the prostate gland can occur due to extreme stress, which my father had definitely suffered in the past several days. I am still not completely sure why this problem was not caught by the hospital staff. However, this condition does not happen suddenly; it builds up over the space of a few days. So, perhaps the timing of his discharge was simply unfortunate.

When I took my father to the urologist a few days later, he said that had Ali not drained my father's bladder that night, it could have caused permanent damage to his urinary system. I was so glad I'd called Ali. I hope my father realizes what a lifesaver he was that day.

Inviting Khalid back to sign the lease

One of my father's first visitors was Khalid. This meeting was a priority for my father because he relies on his rental properties for his living, and I had a feeling that he had become strapped for cash—exacerbated by the fact that scoundrels had depleted all his bank accounts.

Khalid arrived at the house with a vase of flowers. I thought that was a really nice gesture. Khalid only stayed briefly due to my father's condition, but he seemed genuinely concerned and asked what had happened. We dodged the question by suggesting that my father's old age was the culprit. If Khalid had any doubts, he did not express them in the meeting. Perhaps our somewhat vague and generalized description got the message across and told him to resist the urge to probe any further.

My father requested he be given more time to recover before

consummating lease negotiations, and Khalid, having seen my father firsthand, very graciously agreed, saying my father's recovery was more important at the moment.

"Let me know if I can be of assistance in any way," he said as he turned to leave.

I thought the offer was very kind, and my father and I were pleased we had successfully bought more time.

Acting swiftly on attorney's action items

Once my father was home, I wasted little time in moving things forward. My to-do list just kept getting longer. In addition to filing the stay order, I had to help my father file police reports relating to his statement and keep pushing police to find and arrest the culprits (yes, you have to push them). I also had to help him file a suit against Raza. Hopefully, once the police got around to actually doing their jobs, we would soon know the identities of all the kidnappers, and we would need to file suits against them also.

All of these tasks fell on my shoulders because my father's path to recovery was slower than expected, and he was not able to take care of anything himself. On top of all the criminal and legal matters, I was tasked with shuttling him to all doctor appointments thanks to Ali's hatred of driving.

I met with Mr. Iqbal almost every day for guidance on how to proceed with the court and CDA matters. We had to move things quickly and make sure that we were one step ahead of the criminals, so my father was going to have to make personal appearances in court soon. He still had to carry a urination bag around at all times, and it was clear he still felt sick. I wasn't sure he would be able to participate in the grueling court schedule. He looked pale and seemed to be giving up. He would not dress up, even for his important court dates. He always wanted to go in his pajamas, no matter how I protested. He walked slowly and with heavy feet. He just did not seem to be interested in pursuing anything. I was acting as his cheerleader, constantly reminding him that with all those documents in criminals' hands, we needed to move fast and he needed to gather all of his courage.

Why are rangers at my father's house?

Peter had told police during the investigation that Abbas called him on the day of the burglary, February 11, 2016, and made some shocking claims. Abbas had told Peter that he should stay away from the house that day because the Pakistan Rangers were looking for my father. Rangers are an elite unit of the police force in Pakistan—a mid-level force between ordinary police and military police. They are highly specialized and trained to capture dangerous and highly sophisticated criminals only. Rangers show up when regular law enforcement has failed. They don't show up quietly, either, but with a lot of fanfare. They are basically the equivalent of US Marshalls, and just like Marshalls, they knock on your door only once before breaking it down to get who they are after. Mere mention of the Rangers will scare the bejesus out of anyone in Pakistan.

Peter had tried to contact my father and let him know about Abbas's warning, but his cell phone was powered off. Peter got a fishy feeling and realized that something was wrong—though he didn't know exactly what—but there was nothing he could do about it. He called Fiza, and she told him that Dad had personally instructed her also to stay away from the house. That confirmed the request's validity for Peter, so he had stayed away.

When my father was in the hospital, I did my due diligence to corroborate the story about Pakistan Rangers visiting his house. I walked around the neighborhood and asked the security guards I had become familiar with if they remembered seeing any Rangers in the neighborhood that day. None of them could remember any type of law enforcement approaching our house, let alone Rangers. Any operation undertaken by Rangers is typically conducted with a lot of hoopla, and someone certainly would have remembered something. I also told the police about all of this and noted that I thought it was very strange, but I don't think they ever took any action to look into it. Honestly, I didn't push it too hard, myself, because of my father's relationship with Abbas. I knew he would have been offended and angry if I had taken any sort of strong action against his best friend. And, really, I didn't have much concrete evidence to go on anyway. Who was to say that Abbas hadn't heard a rumor that the Rangers were planning a raid?

A suspicious phone conversation with Abbas

My father was deluged with calls from people inquiring after his health, so he asked me to field the calls, providing quick updates to everyone except the select few he wished to speak personally. One of those privileged callers was none other than his Unit 2 tenant, Abbas. Abbas had been calling on a nearly daily basis to inquire after my father ever since he was admitted to the hospital. The calls didn't slow after my father's return home, and Abbas was listed so high in my father's good books that he *always* wanted to receive his phone calls personally.

I, however, still had some mixed feelings about the guy thanks to the whole false alarm with the Rangers, and I had not talked with him since our last conversation in the car on the way back from Shahpur when he had not bothered to help us out with police matters in Islamabad. I had, however, witnessed my father chatting with Abbas on the phone on multiple occasions. Abbas' dedication to those almost daily phone calls began to soften my feelings toward him. I reminded myself that I had not even met the guy and shouldn't hold anything against him.

That was until I had a strange conversation with Abbas myself. Whenever my father slept upstairs, I took to carrying his phone around the house to field calls and keep it from waking him. On one such occasion, Abbas called. When I picked up, he thought I was my father.

"Hello, Mubashar! How are you?"

"This is Syed, his son. I'm attending his phone for the time being."

"How is Mubashar doing?"

"He's making good progress; he should be back to his old self soon."

As my father's good friend, Abbas was privy to the fact that he was actually kidnapped. He expressed his sympathy toward my father and said that what had happened to him was terribly sad. He was very soft-spoken, and he seemed genuinely concerned about my father's wellbeing.

"Yes, I'm working aggressively with the police, and I think we'll get the criminals who did this very soon," I said.

"Good. Good."

"Where are you calling from?"

"I had to come to New York for an emergency assignment from the US Consulate."

"Really? Where in New York?" I asked, to which he replied, "Brooklyn."

I looked at the clock and mentally calculated the present time in New York. It must have been around 5 a.m. This struck me as really odd. Why would someone purportedly on urgent assignment in New York call his landlord in Pakistan first thing in the morning?

I mean, I understood he was a good friend of my father, but waking up at odd hours inquiring after his wellbeing did not bode well with me, especially since this friendship had only developed over the course of the last few months. It wasn't like a close childhood friendship, which might better explain the extreme state of sadness over his buddy's condition and the urgent need to get in touch. Even then, a childhood buddy would probably call at reasonable hours during the day. Something just wasn't adding up in my mind about this guy.

Still, being a positive person, I reminded myself that there are wonderful people in this world who always put others before themselves, and maybe Abbas was one of them. After giving Abbas an update, I informed my father that he had called from New York inquiring about his recovery. My father was delighted to hear that he had such a wonderful friend who cared enough about him to call while on important business in another country.

Doesn't everyone need friends like these in life?

CHAPTER 15

PRIME SUSPECT

You will remember that when I first asked my father in Shahpur police station if he knew of anyone who might want to harm him enough to arrange his kidnapping, torture, and murder, he did not hesitate to mention Riaz Khan's name. We hadn't hesitated to mention his name to police either. My father's history with Riaz Khan is long and sordid.

Since my father owns a lot of property in Islamabad, he is in constant need of upgrades, whether it be because a tenant vacated or just for regular upkeep. He is always on the lookout for trustworthy and able contractors. It is hard to find good labor in Pakistan (or anywhere, really), so hiring and holding onto good contractors is always at the back of my father's mind.

He hired a man named Riaz Khan sometime in 2004 or 2005. Khan started as a day laborer but quickly rose through the ranks to become a general contractor and a valued employee of my father's organization, VIP Global Group. I remember many phone conversations with my father in which he talked highly of this fellow and discussed what a great job he was doing for the firm, but I had never met him in person until my 2016 visit. But before we get to that, let me further explain how Khan achieved this high standing within my father's company.

After seeing Khan's work as a laborer, it hadn't been long before my father started to assign him projects of prime importance, and he proved equal to the task each time. During that same time, a trusted contractor who had been working for my father since 1996 was caught stealing from the company. My father's office secretary, Noor, discovered that invoices provided by this contractor hadn't matched up with inventory for several months. Noor also kept meticulous records of every item purchased on the company's behalf, and the costs were well below the reimbursement amounts requested by this contractor. When confronted, he had admitted his wrongdoing and was fired. I don't know if the theft was reported to police, but I do know that his departure was not a pleasant experience for anyone. Soon after he was let go, he filed numerous lawsuits against my father and even Noor.

The one good outcome of the whole thing was that Khan was ready and willing to fill the fired contractor's shoes.

By 2007, Khan had already become one of my father's right-hand men. During those days, my father was looking for someone to look after one of his commercial properties (commonly referred to as a plaza in Pakistan), which was located in F-10 Markaz. He had owned the building since 1996, when he bought it rather cheap. I don't know the exact sum he obtained it for, but its value has grown exponentially, and now it's worth about Rs. 150,000,000 ($1.5 million US, given the exchange rate in 2016).

The plaza is divided into a four-story hotel space with eleven rooms, and two additional commercial spaces—one about 3,000 sq. ft. and the other about 2,000 sq. ft.

My father was able to rent out the two commercial spaces to two different tenants: a well-known UK fast food chain by the name of Mr. Cod, which is basically a fish burger joint, and Dubai Bank, from which Raza had stolen my father's funds.

When I visited Pakistan back in February 2007, my father was running all the hotel portion's operations himself. However, he was considering leasing the operation to someone else because running a hotel on a daily basis was too much work for him. His idea was to lease the hotel out for a fixed monthly rent and allow the operator to keep all other profits, as he or she would be responsible for day-to-day duties like serving guests, hiring employees, property maintenance, room cleaning, etc. It would be a win-win situation for both parties.

As luck would have it, my father did not have to look far to find a trustworthy operator. Khan agreed to take on the job. He had proven himself to be a hardworking individual who understood my father's business style and who was always ready to take on big challenges. He had proven himself equal to any task that my father assigned to him, so he was the first and most logical choice. There was no doubt in my father's mind that Khan was an excellent fit.

They drafted a lease agreement for five years, and my father made sure the rent was set at an amount that would allow Khan to turn a good profit. Khan proved to be an excellent operator, and my father soon started collecting his monthly payments, while Khan started enjoying healthy profits above and beyond the monthly rent.

The hotel was very well kept, the rooms remained almost fully rented, and the guests were delighted with the service. My father never had any issue collecting his monthly payment, and Khan went out of his way to make sure my father was pleased with his operations. He realized my father had given him the opportunity of a lifetime, and he wasn't going to mess it up. Thanks to my father, Khan had gone from working as an ordinary laborer who had to hop from job to job to make a living to being the owner of a successful hotel. His deal with my father allowed him to take control of his destiny and live the life of his dreams. My father was convinced he had made a good decision and that Khan had "taken the bull the by the horns" and was well on his way to financial success.

The first time I ever heard my father speak negatively about Khan was when he visited me in Chicago in 2011. Hotel operations had deteriorated and his monthly payments had become erratic. In fact, for many months Khan had outright refused to pay him anything, saying business was too slow for the rent to be fair. My father, however, had asked around at other hotels in the vicinity, and everyone had told him that the business in that area could not have been better.

During later conversations with my father after he returned to Pakistan, he told me he had discovered that Khan was running prostitutes and drugs through the hotel.

"How did you find this out?" I asked after I'd recovered from the initial shock.

"Someone from the Islamabad Police got in touch. Apparently, the hotel is a 'hub for numerous illegal activities.'"

According to Pakistani law, because my father was still technically the owner of the hotel, the burden was now on him to stop the illegal activity or risk a police raid and all sorts of legal troubles.

I could tell by my father's voice that he was furious and more than a little exasperated with the whole thing. Accepting rent for the hotel rather than running it was meant to make his life easier and to give someone else an unbelievable opportunity. Instead, he had been betrayed by the very person he had sought to help and found himself in a giant mess that he would have to clean up. The police knew that my father had nothing to do with the actual illegal activities, and he was not personally charged with any wrongdoing, but his name on the property title laid the burden of eradicating the illegal activities squarely on his shoulders for the sake of the property and his investment. My father went round and round with Khan over the next several months, demanding he cease and desist all illegal activity on the property. My father could not kick Khan out of the hotel due to the five-year lease, but reversely, Khan could not engage in unsavory activities per the lease terms. I never understood why police bothered my father and laid the responsibility on him instead of just arresting Khan and stopping all the activities that way. To me, this seemed like a shady attempt by Pakistani police to drag an innocent party into a messy situation to see if they could get some bribes thrown their way to rectify the matter. Needless to say, my father's frustration grew day by day, and his relationship with Khan was irrevocably severed. Khan remained bull-headed and refused to give up his prostitutes and his drugs.

The only silver lining was that the hotel lease was coming due in the middle of 2012. My father had told Khan in no uncertain terms that he was not going to renew the lease. Khan did not react well, and many unpleasant exchanges (some in person) took place over the course of many months. For instance, one day my father took a police inspector to confront Khan directly at the hotel. Khan did not admit to any wrongdoing, and the policeman just gave him a warning. Later that day, Khan called my father and threatened that if he ever dared to bring police onto the premises without proof, he would be sorry. Another time, he asked my father to meet at a neutral location to deliver the lease check after months of delay. They ended up having a heated conversation in which Khan claimed my father should not be calling again and again asking for rent. My father, of course, asked him just what did he think he should do when rent was several months late? Throughout the whole argument, Khan had a bodyguard looming behind him in an attempt to intimidate my father. I was privy to the whole situation via regular phone conversations with my father.

My father had not seen a single penny from his hotel property in months, even though various sources told him that the hotel operation was extremely profitable for Khan. Not only was he making money from legally renting the hotel space, but he was also raking in money from his illegal endeavors. He appeared addicted to his dangerous lifestyle. I am sure greed & avarice played a key role as well. In just a few years, Khan had gone from a poor day laborer to something of a small-time crime boss swimming in money. However, when people don't handle their newfound wealth responsibly, they often end up worse than before. I think as soon as he started making money legally from the hotel operations, he attracted the wrong sort of company, and everything went downhill from there.

Now Khan's downfall was fast approaching, and he knew it. He would be kicked out of the hotel and would soon become a riches to rags story in the eyes of his family and friends. Khan would soon have to go back to his old temporary labor jobs, as in all likelihood he didn't have enough saved up to sustain himself. More often than not, when people indulge in self-destructive, self-satisfying lifestyles, they blow all their money and have little to show when it comes to actual savings. Thus, a very bleak and poverty-filled future was staring Khan right in the face, and he was already starting to see dark clouds on the horizon. Police were preparing a case against him, and they had ample evidence. So, not only was he going to lose the lease on the hotel, he was going to jail… if he didn't take action.

Forging a fake agreement

One day, after my father finished a hearty breakfast at home and went into his home office to begin his day, the special court mail carrier delivered a summons for my father. Khan had filed a lawsuit against him that claimed he was non-compliant with the lease agreement extension executed between the two parties.

In a surprisingly bold move, Khan had caught my father completely off guard by obtaining the services of a corrupt attorney (and distant relative of his) who forged a fake agreement, which stated, "Mr. Mubashar has extended the lease agreement of his hotel property with Mr. Khan for another five years and has received a compensation of Rs. 2,500,000 ($25,000 US) in exchange of extending this agreement."

None of it was true.

My father was flabbergasted when he found out that Khan had committed this type of blatant fraud against him. Khan, however, did not stop there. In another surprisingly bold move, he sued my father in the superior court to try and enforce that very forged agreement. As a result of the filing of this suit, Khan was granted an injunction that stopped all payments of the hotel rent until all court matters were settled.

Now my father all of a sudden found himself playing defense, proving to the court that everything Khan was saying was false.

In a country like Pakistan, with a defunct judiciary and weak law and order, it is relatively easy to create such ambiguity and confusion in order to buy time. Courts are required to hear every case. However, it takes such a long time for courts to reach a decision that even if you win in the end, it is hard to receive adequate compensation for all the time and resources that were wasted in fighting that battle. You win the battle, lose the war. What do a criminal and his attorney lose by showing up court date after court date? Nothing really; he only wins himself more time to continue his desired activities. Whereas a decent citizen who has other productive things to do with his life is put through hell.

Thus Khan's game plan was, in lieu of winning—which was highly unlikely—to get away basically scot-free by handing over the keys and getting out with all the money made from hotel operations during the court process. He had already been granted a stop on all payments; so perhaps he figured the court system would work in his favor for the rest of the case. However, my father countersued, and though the case dragged on for about a year, the FIA deemed the lease agreement forged in late 2014, and my father won his own case. As a result, Khan was arrested and sentenced to eighteen months in prison for forgery.

However, Khan served only eight months in jail, and was released toward the end of 2015. And since my father was kidnapped in February 2016, he had a strong reason to believe that Khan had something to do with it.

Khan's corrupt attorney

Although he had already served eight months in prison, the case regarding his forged signature on the lease renewal was still ongoing in court. The latest court date was fast approaching, and both my father and Khan had to present themselves in front of a judge. The only reason this case was still dragging on was because of Khan's corrupt attorney. Technically speaking, Khan had yet to hand over "legal" possession of the hotel property to my father. So the obvious question is how can a person who has already been convicted and served time for illegal possession of property get away with refusing to vacate that same premises?

Khan's attorney was arguing that forgery was a criminal offence and vacating the premises was a civil issue, so the courts must treat the two issues separately. To our surprise and chagrin, the judge was allowing that to happen. Khan's attorney had already gone head to head with Mr. Iqbal in two separate court sessions, arguing that Khan had been convicted and served his time *only* for forgery, which had nothing to do with illegal possession. Thus, Khan should maintain ownership until proven guilty of illegal possession. However, Mr. Iqbal countered that the very reason forgery was committed was for the purpose of illegal possession, so the conviction automatically called for vacating the premises, effective immediately. Mr. Iqbal argued that Khan's conviction and sentence automatically made the argument for two separate cases (forgery and illegal possession) moot. At one point, Mr. Iqbal became so frustrated with going around and around with this stupid argument that, right in front of the judge, he looked to Khan's attorney and, exasperated, said,

"Why don't you just shoot me in the head now?"

If Mr. Iqbal could just convince the judge that there were not two separate cases here, Khan would have been forced to hand over possession right there in court, giving the keys back to my father in the presence of the judge. However, Mr. Iqbal could never bring the argument to a conclusion, so this handing over of possession hadn't taken place, and technically Khan still had the possession of the hotel property. This ongoing legal battle with Khan was definitely a possible motive for my father's kidnapping, and we all felt that Khan needed to be questioned.

This corrupt attorney was reaping plenty of benefits throughout the whole process, too. He had looked after the hotel operations, though somewhat indirectly, during the eight months Khan was in jail.

I was completely flabbergasted when my father explained to me how Khan's attorney was still manipulating this situation in the courts even after conviction. But I understood the idea behind this concocted litigation: to tie up the case in courts while reaping the financial rewards all along the way. And so what if he lost the battle in the end? He had already done his time; he would just have to hand over the keys, not the finances gained during the court proceedings.

I was convinced this attorney was as much a foe as Khan.

CHAPTER 16

TWO BUMBLING COPS AND A MOTORBIKE

The next natural step after we'd thoroughly explained this history to authorities was for police to seek Khan out for further questioning. Easier said than done.

I got together with the Kohsar inspector to discuss his next course of action. Now I don't know if he was really extraordinarily busy or just pretending to be, but it seemed to me that his progress was painfully slow. Whenever I ask him to follow up on something, he would either say that he was on some other police assignment that day or that he did not have access to a police vehicle. On quite a few occasions, I had to haul him around myself to get anything done. One of my most frequent requests was that he take steps to arrest Raza since we had already identified her. The Kohsar inspector told me that he ran a background check using her NIC (National Identity Card) and found that her permanent address was in Karachi, some 1500 kilometers (about 932 miles) away from Islamabad. He told me that the station did not have the resources to make an out-of-town arrest and that if we really wanted him and his men to go and "knock on doors" in Karachi, we must be prepared to pick up the tab. This would include, but not be limited to, arranging flights and hotel rooms, along with daily meals and other expenses along the way. I imagined a bottomless pit opening its wide mouth in the middle of the earth, ready to devour our money. Plus there was no guarantee that Raza was even living at the residence listed on the NIC. I had a feeling that police would make a "tour de grand" of Karachi on our dime and then come back empty-handed. It wasn't going to happen.

Then, like a lightening flash, an idea came to me. I knew from my meeting with Phoenix Security that anyone's location can be easily tracked using cell phone signals, so I asked the Kohsar inspector to track Raza's location that way. The inspector said he'd get right on it. It took him another two days to get back to me.

"She's got three cell phones registered in her name, and all of them have been disconnected," he said when he called me at last.

My epiphany turned out to be a dead end.

I vented to my father about my displeasure and frustration with how the Kohsar inspector was dawdling around our case and sniffing around our wallets for bribes. To my surprise, my father asked me to keep my head down and avoid pissing him off.

"That's how police in Pakistan operate, and rubbing them the wrong way will only backfire," he said.

"You think we should try to bribe him?"

"Possibly, but our best bet right now is to just keep working with the guy and try not to upset him," he said. "And be extra careful. Everyone around here thinks expatriates are extra rich. They'll consider milking money out of you a moral obligation."

Since police claimed their hands were tied on Raza's arrest, I next asked them if they could focus solely on Khan.

"That's a good idea," the Kohsar inspector said, eyebrows raised like this was the first time the idea had ever crossed his mind. "We'll start looking for him immediately."

I thought to myself that a tenth grader would make a better police officer than this guy, but I held my tongue. Instead, I made it my duty to pressure him to get himself in gear and arrest Khan, who was at least local and potentially easier to locate. If arrested, he could hopefully shed some light on the situation. My father, at least, was convinced that Khan had either played a direct role or somehow indirectly influenced the kidnapping, say by providing personal information to the kidnappers.

The problem was that we had no idea where to find Khan. We had his cell phone number, but we didn't know where he lived. My father said that Khan still showed up at the hotel from time to time because his gang was still running hotel operations, and other nefarious business dealings. So, I asked the police to stake out the hotel to look for Khan, but there was a problem: neither the police nor I knew what Khan looked like!

My father did not have any pictures, and he was too ill to be hauled around. The only person among us who could identify Khan was good old Peter. He had worked with Khan on some of my father's projects. I asked the Kohsar inspector if he could take Peter to the hotel and try to make an arrest. However, I heard nothing for days.

Police want to make an arrest using my car

The next time I marched back into the Kohsar police station to get some answers from the inspector—Peter ready and waiting in the car—he was still full of excuses and drama.

"I'm sorry, but I don't have a vehicle today," he said with a shrug. "It was assigned to an emergency earlier this morning. If you want me to make that arrest today, you can drive me and one of my men down to the hotel in your car." He smiled. "We'll make the arrest, shove him in your backseat, and bring him back here, no problem."

I didn't have any more time to waste, so I agreed. I drove the armed inspector, one of the constables (also armed), and Peter to the hotel.

"Park the car a safe distance from the building, but make sure you have a good view of the front entrance," the inspector said as we pulled into the lot.

We were reasonably camouflaged among the sea of cars in the plaza. Since none of us could recognize Khan except Peter, we were relying on him to alert us whenever he got a glimpse of the suspect. However, Khan would also recognize Peter, so we didn't want him to roam around the hotel and accidentally alert Khan to anything odd. Since both police officers were in their uniforms, they would set off even louder alarm bells. That left me. I floated the idea of going inside the hotel and posing as a guest asking about room rates, but I decided it would be a pretty useless plan since I wouldn't even recognize Khan. All I'd have to share when I came back out were the room rates. In the end, it was decided that I would just circle around the hotel and report back anything of significance to the police. I made a quick loop around the building and came back with nothing.

Please see the picture of the hotel entrance below, which I took while walking around looking for any suspicious activity. (Sometimes, don't you want to thank whoever invented the camera phone?)

Actual photo I took of the entrance to the hotel property. (Date: March 2016, Source: Author)

We sat in the car for an hour, and nothing was happening. It was about 10 a.m., and the plaza wasn't too busy that day. I drove around the hotel and came back to the same spot where we again sat looking out the windows for Khan as he entered or exited the hotel.

It wasn't long before I started to sense that this could be a big waste of time and an inappropriate way to make an arrest. What if Khan never showed up at the hotel that day? What if he already knew his former boss had been kidnapped and that there was a possibility that he would be named a suspect? If Khan was actually the mastermind behind the kidnapping, he would definitely know all about it, and this hotel would be the last place he would visit. I mentioned my reservations to the inspector and constable.

"Yeah…" said the inspector, nodding slowly. "Yeah, that makes a lot of sense."

I wasn't sure whether to laugh or groan. I was doing all the police work here!

"Can't you just locate him through his cell phone?" I asked. "You have the number on record, right?"

"Yeah, I do. That's a good idea."

While I tried not to roll my eyes, the inspector called his contact at the cell phone company who used to do location tracking for Islamabad Police. After he hung up, he told me that it would take another couple of hours for his contact to trace Khan's location.

Who's eavesdropping?

Right after the call was made, Peter said, "Hey, you see that guy on the motorbike? He's been there a while, and he keeps looking over here."

We all turned our heads as casually as possible. Sure enough, there he was, a younger guy with a moustache and long hair. When his eyes flicked to our car, we all turned away or acted like we didn't notice him. We observed him for a few minutes and witnessed him make several phone calls. Every now and then, we'd catch him watching us.

"I don't like this guy," said the constable.

"His behavior is quite concerning," said the inspector.

"It's like he's giving somebody live updates on us or something," I said after about a half hour of this.

After yet another half hour dragged by with no change, our patience ran out.

"This is ridiculous," said the inspector, "Circle around the plaza, and park in the back."

I obliged and found a spot behind the plaza where we could still see the traffic flow, but we were not in plain sight.

The revving of a motorbike engine made us all exchange looks of amazement. The same guy appeared around the side of the plaza and parked his bike a safe distance from us, where he unabashedly continued observing our car.

"This guy's up to no good," said Peter.

I thought Peter had nailed it on the head, but the inspector and his subordinate went round and round exchanging theories about what this guy might be up to.

"Think we should get out and say something to him?" said the constable.

"Not sure it's appropriate," said the inspector. "We're not in a police vehicle."

We waited and watched. The biker was still making regular phone calls.

"Shouldn't you go confront him?" I asked.

"No, no. Not yet. Let's see what happens," said the inspector.

The motorbike didn't budge.

"Alright, that's it!" said the inspector. "Move the car again. If he follows us to a third location, we're making an arrest."

I did as he asked. From our new location in a neighboring plaza, we vigilantly watched out the windows, but the guy and his bike were nowhere to be seen. We waited for a few more minutes to make sure. There were audible sighs of relief, and the tension inside the car ebbed quite a bit.

At this point, we were just sitting in the wrong plaza shooting the breeze. I could not believe I was hauling these guys around in the first place, especially if they weren't going to do their job. I had enough on my plate without babysitting the police. Finally, my patience ran out, and I asked the inspector to call his phone operator contact again.

Knowing that I was stuck with these guys at least for today, I got out and took a walk around shops to calm down.

A sign reading, "We sell Pokémon cards," caught my eye. Before I left the US, my son had asked me to bring him back Pokémon cards, so I went into the shop and bought him a whole bunch.

Can you arrest Khan, please?

When the Kohsar inspector finally received a text from his contact, we discovered Khan was currently in a town by the name of Qutbal, about thirty minutes away from Islamabad. The source even knew the names of the street corners Khan was walking past at that moment.

"Great!" I said. "Let's go get him!"

"Uh, hold on," said the inspector. "Qutbal is out of our jurisdiction. We'll need to go back to the station and work this out with my senior officer."

It was clear we wouldn't make an arrest that day. But at least Peter and I didn't have to waste any more time hanging around the hotel.

"How long will it take to get the proper permissions?" I asked.

"Two to three days."

This made me nervous. Khan might move on to the next town in the next couple of days. Then what? Would it take another couple of days to get appropriate permissions for *that* location? The way this inspector was operating was making me paranoid. I was never sure if anything he said was real or just made up to siphon a bribe from me. I couldn't devote any more energy to figuring it out at that moment, and I did not want to set up the wrong pattern by offering him a reward when he had accomplished nothing. One thing was sure, though; I was rapidly losing confidence in his abilities.

I mean, could he really just be that stupid? I simply did not have that answer. All I knew for sure was that even now, when Khan's location was known, he was showing no urgency to make an arrest. This was just ridiculous to me, but there was little I could do. Though we were done for the day, I still treated the policemen to lunch and dropped them off at the station afterward.

CHAPTER 17

IT'S NOT WHO YOU ARE, IT'S WHO YOU KNOW

Against the recommendation of the security company, I had decided to live with my father in his house. I was not the only one staying with him; Fiza and her son were there every day, too. The security company had repeatedly told us that we were making a grave mistake by doing this. Their logic was that the house was a major target, and no one should be living there. If, for some reason, my father must live in the house, they warned that the whole family shouldn't be staying there regularly, because it would be very easy for criminals to "take care" of everyone in one spot.

As much as these warnings frightened us, certain limitations got in the way of following this advice through. Fiza's place was too small, and Ali was studying for an exam late at night because he had to work during the day. I did not have another place to live except a hotel, and I was on a limited budget. Good hotels don't come cheap in Pakistan. Second, my father had made it clear to everyone that he was not going anywhere, even if it killed him. Fiza had to spend the better part of her days at our father's house because she was looking after him as his personal doctor.

Taking into consideration our father's health and our inability to relocate the whole family, vacating the house was not an option, but we did ensure that we took extraordinary steps for our safety. With the help of Phoenix Security, the best-known security company in Islamabad, we had secured the house very well against attack. Security was present 24/7, with one armed guard present during the daytime and another one throughout the night. The guards were armed with semi-automatic rifles at all times. There were many other houses on the block that had their own armed security guards, so we took some solace that a full blown attack in an area that was (supposedly) so secure would be highly unlikely. Furthermore, I had walked around and begun to build a rapport with all the security guards in the neighborhood, and many agreed to "keep an eye" on our house indirectly. Overall, we felt that establishing personal security in addition to the general security around the block was adequate enough to thwart any type of attack.

Having armed guards is in fashion

It was actually heartbreaking to witness the state of affairs in the neighborhood where I grew up. Once looked upon as completely safe, it now seemed to be a place where everyone was concerned about their safety. As I walked down the block, security guards with hulking shoulders, bulges at their hips, and rifles strapped to their backs followed my progress with grave eyes. They looked like soldiers, with black or deep green camouflaged uniforms, army caps, and large boots. The front yards of the fine houses were marred by small, bunker-type structures erected for the security guards as a place to sit down, eat meals, and pass the day. These bunkers are typically eight feet by five feet structures only big enough to house a chair and table, a small radio, and a water-cooler. The very presence of these bunkers works as a deterrent against burglary and any other criminal activity.

And in all honestly, things are usually quiet in affluent neighborhoods like my father's; it's not as if there are shootings or other types of attacks happening on a daily basis. Personal security is a preventive measure to avoid any mischief in the first place, to keep it from slinking in from the surrounding neighborhoods. Personal security is basically an expensive showoff tactic to protect yourself *before* someone even thinks of harming you. Sadly, general law and order in Pakistan has deteriorated in the last decade, and people who can afford it feel they have to take security measures on their own.

Seeing the change hurts. The neighborhood was a joy to grow up in during the mid-1980s and the 1990s, and all of my best childhood memories were made there. There were never any security guards standing outside houses while we kids played cricket and soccer in the streets. Our parents felt so secure that they used to let us out on our own at night. I remember numerous nights spent sitting outside the houses with friends, laughing and telling jokes with the stars overhead. Neighbors looked out for each other; there was no need for security guards.

In 2016, things were completely different. The escalating fear and security concerns among the public caused a mushrooming of security companies in Islamabad. Before the 2000s, only government offices or sensitive institutions like foreign missions hired security outside their buildings. Now security firms seem to be some of the most profitable businesses in Islamabad. And that's just in the capital city, which is widely considered the safest in the country. Imagine the circumstances in other cities such as Lahore or Karachi where shootings and murders are not even newsworthy nowadays.

Sorry, there is no electricity

As I worked on my father's affairs, I slowly adjusted back to life in Pakistan, but one thing that never failed to annoy me was the load-shedding. You may remember that the Shahpur police station was in total darkness when we first arrived thanks to this practice in which the power is cut off regularly to relieve the overburdened power grid. In Islamabad, the power is cut for one hour every three hours. The hour-long cutoff occurs in different sectors at different times so that the whole city isn't plunged into darkness at once. The heating and cooling systems rely on electricity, so whenever the power goes out, you are left without heat in winter and air conditioning in summer. Just imagine how much misery this can add for someone who is sick, like my father. It's a huge problem for everyone, which is why power generators are highly sought after in Pakistan, but not everyone can afford them. Typically big businesses have them, but small businesses and common citizens usually just have to deal with the constant power outages. Whenever the power was out, it would cause sudden changes in temperature. I had to pile blankets on top of my father when it got too cold and try to let in some air when it got too hot. The constant back and forth only made him sicker and more miserable.

Load-shedding slows everything down, including my progress with my father's affairs. Just when I would start to make urgent photocopies of important documents, the lights would go out. Then I'd have to either drive to another sector and find a photocopy machine or sit around for an hour, waiting for the power.

As March progressed, so did my father's condition. Mr. Iqbal began to request my father's presence in court so that we could move everything along before the criminals made attempts to sell his assets to unwitting buyers. My father hesitated at first, but after I told him how important the matter was and encouraged him to gather all his strength, he reluctantly agreed.

During those days, many people came to see my father and wish him a speedy recovery. Some of them were acquaintances whom my father had approached for help because of their connections with government agencies. The idea was to stir up all the contacts we possibly could so that we left no stone unturned in the case. One such acquaintance was well-connected within the Federal Investigation Agency (FIA), and he promised to ask FIA officers to look into the matter and try to locate the culprits via their additional resources. My father also invited an attorney who had contacts with provincial police. I was not too sure what sort of help he could provide, but I followed my father's direction and accommodated his visits whenever he wanted. My father was not in good enough health to have long meetings, so I also became his personal assistant, fielding who was allowed to see him and when.

Multi-tasking or multi-multi-tasking

All throughout April and May 2016 I helped my father with doctor appointments, dealt with police, dealt with the courts, held meetings with our attorney, and worked with the CDA to thwart the malicious transfer of property behind our backs. At my father's behest, I wrote multiple letters to a wide array of agencies requesting help on multiple fronts. I sent in multiple applications to the Supreme Court's Overseas Pakistani complaint wing that can expedite matters for overseas visitors who feel they are stuck in the country due to slow court proceedings. I was using my US Citizenship to my advantage and seeking help to expedite my father's court cases so that I could go back to the US with some peace of mind. However, as with all judicial matters in Pakistan, it was like pulling teeth to get anyone to respond or take action. I sent far more applications than typical and also made multiple trips to the Supreme Court to try and get some answers. When I at last got a staff member to give me the time of day, though, it didn't exactly turn out as I'd hoped.

"Just who are you seeking expedited services for, sir?" the employee asked, studying me closely over the counter. "Yourself or your father?"

"Well, it's my father's case, but he's taken ill because of the torture his kidnappers put him through. Right now I'm taking care of everything, and I need this expedited so that I can return home to the US for work and for my family."

"Your father was the only one kidnapped, yes? Not you?"

"Yes, but—"

"Then, I'm very sorry, but we cannot expedite the case. Your father is not a foreigner. The matter will have to move through the system in the regular manner."

I opened my mouth for one last try, but another employee walked in and saw me at that moment.

With a half-smile on his face, he said, "You again? You're very dedicated." He chuckled. "What exactly are you trying to do here? Understand how the Supreme Court works?"

I laughed along with him while the other employee raised a curious eyebrow, but I quickly went on my way after that. The last thing I needed was any sort of rumor spreading to authorities that

I was spying on the inner workings of the Supreme Court. It seems ludicrous, but suspicions can grow on a whim in Pakistan.

I next wrote to high-ranking police officials such as the Senior Superintendent of Police and the Inspector General of Police, who is the highest authority in the whole police force. I also wrote to the Chief of the Federal Investigation Agency (FIA), which is like the CIA in the US. I even wrote a letter to the Chief of the Army Staff at the time, General Raheel Sharif, who is the highest authority within the Pakistani military.[13]

All the above letters were sent out with certified mail, but sadly, I did not hear back from anyone, at least not while I was in Pakistan.

By the end of March, my father was inviting more and more well-connected people from his circle of acquaintances to discuss his situation and seek advice. I had not met any of them in the past and had to take my father's word for it that they were all trustworthy. I sat in on almost all these meetings to try to get to know these people.

One meeting, I remember, was with a gentleman who had worked at the FIA in the past but who now had his own consulting practice for people dealing with complex matters involving law enforcement. He was accompanied by another gentleman, who had done some real estate business with my father in the past. The most painful thing for me was that during every meeting I had to listen to the story of my father's kidnapping and torture. Each time, my eyes found his urine bag, and my anger bubbled to the surface.

The gentleman with FIA contacts expressed a lot of sympathy for my father and told him that he knew some high-ranking officials who would be willing to help him. He said that the official he wanted

---

[13] Sharif was succeeded by Qamar Javed Bajwa in November 2016.

to contact first was out of town, but he would get in touch with him as soon as he was back to arrange a meeting for us.

FIA involvement would be a tremendous help because, as a government agency, it has far more resources than local police thanks to the extra funds it receives from the federal government. The FIA has better technology and various office branches spread throughout the country that are all well connected via computer networks. Raza had a permanent address in the city of Karachi, so the FIA's ability to communicate across jurisdictions would have been very helpful. Local police's lack of such resources was apparent in their inability to make any substantial progress. I think their biggest problem was locating a criminal who had committed a crime in Islamabad and then escaped elsewhere (say, to Karachi, the largest city in Pakistan). There is no established means of communication between different city's police stations, so the Islamabad and Karachi police would have no way to coordinate and figure out the whereabouts of said criminal. Should Raza be identified in Karachi during routine police encounters such as a traffic stop, no connection would be made because police don't have a centralized database. The FIA, on the other hand, can often locate a fugitive rather quickly through their intercity communications and interconnected systems with other government branches. The FIA has better "mouse traps" with which to catch criminals who move across the country. It even has the means to catch criminals at the airport should they try to flee, or enter, the country. Given the type of criminals we were dealing with, I knew it was necessary to involve more sophisticated law enforcement.

But why did we have to ask for help from insider acquaintances to get the attention of law enforcement agencies in Pakistan? Isn't it their job to catch dangerous criminals? Well, the answer is not very simple and also very subjective. Every agency claims that they don't have enough funds and that they are starved of resources due to the government's limited budget. They have to prioritize their case load, and they typically attend to the most serious cases first. But my question to them would be, isn't kidnapping serious enough? Due to the high rates of corruption in Pakistani law enforcement, you never know whether an agency is really resource starved or just not moving forward because they are waiting on "tips" to give them incentive. This makes things complicated because you are never sure where you stand with these authorities. Good luck getting anything done in Pakistan unless you know someone who knows someone at a particular agency or you have a lot of funds to blow. This type of environment only breeds more criminal activity because criminals know if they find the right official, they can always pay their way out of trouble. Criminals hope that by playing the system, they can burn out their victims so much that they just give up their pursuit.

All the delays created by authorities were my major concern while I was in Pakistan. I had a limited timeframe in which I was trying to complete the maximum number of tasks, but I faced delays on every front. The most frustrating thing was that I had to constantly gauge which of these delays were makeshift and which ones were real. I was advised by my father to resist mentioning that I was a visitor from the US because then the officials might try to use this to their advantage by creating more hurdles and attempting to extort funds from me.

Seeking assistance from anyone

As I have already mentioned, the most powerful institution in Pakistan is the military. The army has the best resources of any agency, making it the most efficient in Pakistan by far. Everyone knows once the Pakistani military gets involved, things get done in a hurry.[14]

The most elite branch of Pakistan's army is Inter-Services Intelligence (ISI). The inner workings of ISI are kept secret, but this unit is known to carry out the most complex tasks in the country. ISI works side by side with the government on top-level security issues and is responsible for creating a roadmap for the foreign policy of Pakistan. ISI is heavily involved in sensitive issues such as terrorism. My point is that once ISI gets involved in a case, consider it a done deal.

Normally, ISI would not get involved in the kidnapping of an ordinary citizen, which has nothing to do with national security. But in Pakistan, it all comes down to who you know. When the army speaks, everyone listens. Thus if you're not getting anywhere with your case, a phone call to the right government agency from the right high-ranking military official can get things done in a hurry. Getting someone to advocate for my father on a military level was a long shot, but given how painfully slow things were moving, I was willing to give anything a try.

It has become a sort of joke in Pakistan that anyone with relatives in ISI will always get justice. That's why very early on in the process I was trying to find an acquaintance who at least knew someone at ISI, or any high-ranking military official for that matter. Our FIA

---

[14] The negative consequence of the extreme power given to the military is that, in the past, it has imposed martial law whenever it deemed the elected civilian government dysfunctional. Martial law simply means dissolving the democratic government currently in place and replacing it with military rule.

acquaintance had turned out to be a dud. First, he put me off for two or three weeks, saying his acquaintance was on vacation, then on a business trip. Maybe he was delaying on purpose so that I would bring him a payment. But when I did not talk about funds, he simply stopped returning my phone calls. So, my father and I were even keener to find a contact within the military.

We caught a possible break in a rather miraculous fashion. A new house was going up on a vacant lot just across the street from us. When I came home one day, I saw two gentlemen watching the construction, and I paused to say hello. They turned out to be father and son, and they were the owners of the new house. In an astonishing chance encounter, the father was not only a retired army officer, he was a high-ranking lieutenant general, just one notch below a general, which is one of the most powerful military positions. Even after retirement, high-ranking military officials typically remain well connected to their junior officers still in service. By Pakistan's standards, this gentleman was a serious big shot, and I became excited. I told my father about my short encounter with our neighbors-to-be. He told me to invite them to the house next time I saw them.

A few days later, the father–son duo showed up at our house. My father was still toting his urine bag around. I think our guests were surprised and perhaps a bit alarmed to see my father in that condition. My father sat down with them and briefly told them his story without going into too much detail. My father mentioned to the retired lieutenant general how little police had done for him and that he needed a "bigger push" to get things rolling. He also talked about his unsuccessful efforts to involve the FIA. There was a desperate plea in my father's voice as he asked our guest if he could perhaps get in touch with someone within the military or ISI who could locate these criminals. The lieutenant general conceded that he did know some senior-level officials at ISI and hinted he would look into the situation further.

I did not have a good feeling though about the meeting when it was over. The two visitors abruptly cut the discussion short after my father's request for assistance. However, they did offer to exchange phone numbers before leaving.

I wasn't sure what to make of their behavior. They did not ask us to provide any sort of evidence or further information to support our case. I also wasn't sure if ISI could even get involved in kidnapping cases like this. In any case, my father asked me to keep in touch with them. His desperation showed in his eagerness to plead his case in front of anyone who would be willing to listen.

Today, when I look back, I realize that our increasing frustration and feelings of helplessness caused us to make a classis mistake. We asked far too much of these people without building any rapport first. Without any knowledge of our family, they couldn't even be sure why my father was kidnapped. For all they knew, we could have had some kind of family feud (which is commonplace in Pakistan), and my father was the victim of revenge. How would they know that my father was an innocent victim? Plus, in my opinion, they probably started to feel unsure about their new neighborhood thanks to our story. These thoughts must have created a lot of negative energy that probably made them feel pretty awkward during our meeting.

When I tried to contact the son a few days later, he just brushed me off, saying he was busy and would call me back. He never did. My father also attempted to contact the father, but he did not get a positive response either. One day while roaming around a nearby market, I ran into the son again. He greeted me, and we had a little chit chat. He told me that his father had contacted someone, and he would let me know the outcome soon. He never got back to me, though. After a couple of weeks or so, both my father and I had lost hope that they would do anything for us. It was time to just move on.

Hitting dead ends like this was becoming quite frustrating and disheartening. I came to realize my best bet was to just keep working with the people I was already involved with, which were mostly police personal, and keep trying to move things forward the old-fashioned way.

By the end of March, Mr. Iqbal had obtained a stay order. This would add an extra hurdle for anyone trying to sell my father's property. Of course, court itself is actually a big hurdle for criminals because, thankfully, bribing a court is still far-fetched in Pakistan.

Obtaining that stay order was no easy task, though. Reason being, my father did not have any proof that he was actually the owner of his property because he no longer had the titles in his possession. He managed to locate photocopies of the titles to some of his properties but not all.

The court hearing to obtain the stay order took place at 9 a.m. on March 7, 2016. My father, Mr. Iqbal, Peter, and I stood together in the courtroom. It was very similar to a typical courtroom in the US. The judge's desk was elevated over a staircase, and his clerk sat at his side. You had to look up to see the judge, which was pretty intimidating, as he never cracked a smile.

The judge asked Mr. Iqbal to present the title documents for the properties the stay order would protect. When Mr. Iqbal explained that all the documents were stolen and that we lacked proof of ownership, the judge became quite agitated. His forehead wrinkled into little frown lines, and he appraised us with a look that clearly said, "Are you out of your mind?"

"You must have *some* proof, or else why are you here at all?" he said.

I presented the photocopies of the few title documents we could find, and the judge quickly agreed to issue a stay for those properties... but only those.

That was going to be a big problem for us. The property title documents were obviously stolen for malicious reasons, and Mr. Iqbal had already warned us that illegal property transfers might have already been taking place behind my father's back. We needed to make sure that we had all stops in place sooner rather than later. If the judge didn't grant us a stay on the remaining properties now, we would have to obtain duplicate title documents from the CDA, which could take months.

My father got up from his chair, urine bag in hand, and made a direct appeal to the judge.

"Your Honor, I have been victimized again and again. Ripped from my home, tortured, my property and possessions stolen from me. The police aren't helping. This stay order is my only way to protect myself from further victimization. Please, if you could kindly render me this favor, I would greatly appreciate it."

Mr. Iqbal stepped in next to give the judge the whole account of the kidnapping and the burglary in which the papers were stolen. Although the judge expressed some sympathy toward my father after learning of his health condition and listening to the kidnapping details, he still insisted that he needed to see proof of ownership before issuing a stay order for the additional properties. Mr. Iqbal argued back that getting duplicate title documents from the

CDA could take months, during which the criminals would doubtless attempt an illegal transfer. He explained the circular reasoning set forth by the judge. He argued that the whole reason we were requesting a stay was to stop property transfer right away. If we could afford to wait a month, then we would not need a stay in the first place. The judge, however, remained firm.

Mr. Iqbal spent a few more minutes trying to convince him, but at the same time, he wanted to avoid coming across as argumentative in court. When the judge showed no signs of budging, he was forced to give up. However, his arguments hadn't fallen on totally deaf ears. Though the laws tied his hands on the stay order, the judge did realize that we had a point. He also knew that obtaining duplicates would take time. So, he did us a favor and told us that if we went to the tax authority and obtained a property tax bill showing my father as the owner on record for those properties and brought it back, he would rehear our case.

My friends, nothing is easy in Pakistan. I was put through the wringer at the tax authority. Long story short, it took me three full work days of standing around in government offices from 8 a.m. to 4 p.m. every day, pleading with clerks to just give us the tax bill. When we finally had it in hand, Mr. Iqbal made another appointment with the judge, who did us another favor by allowing us that special court session. We all traipsed down to the court again and presented the tax bill to the judge, who at last issued the stay order, freezing all property transfers without court permission and my father's presence. Only a court authority can authorize the removal of the stay from the files, which gave us significant peace of mind.

My work was far from over, though. Now, with stay order in hand, the next task was to deliver it to the CDA (Capital Development Authority). The day after getting the stay, I showed up at the CDA as soon as the doors opened, and I had more surprises in store. Properly submitting the stay order proved just as difficult as obtaining it. Once again making a long story short, it took me a good two days of running back and forth before I finally succeeded in submitting it.

At long last, we had stopped any chance of illegal property transfer. My father and I shared a collective sigh of relief. But we still weren't done. Mr. Iqbal suggested my father transfer all his assets into his children's names in order to avoid ownership issues further down the road.

You see, we had only stopped the chance of the kidnappers trying to transfer the properties into their names or an unwitting buyer's name. However, the chance of them doing that had been small to begin with. Because my father had survived their attack, they surely realized we were on high alert. It would have been downright stupid on their part just to show up in court with a willing buyer and attempt to transfer the property. Anyone who came forward with these stolen documents would be deemed a culprit automatically.

Our biggest and main fear, however, was that these criminals would attempt to sell the properties to multiple buyers at once, only hanging around long enough to get the earnest money before disappearing, as I described in chapter nine. At some point, the people they scammed would come looking for the owner, my father. With no other recourse available to them, the buyers would blame my father and most likely sue him.

To mitigate the fallout, Mr. Iqbal wanted my father to distribute his estate to his children by transferring his titles to us. That way, he would not remain the legal owner, and if the scammers collected earnest money on the properties using the titles that carried my father's name, he could avoid conflict with the defrauded buyers by saying he no longer owned the property. We also hoped that the criminals would find out one way or another that my father was not the legal owner of the properties anymore, thwarting such mischief altogether.

Well, live and learn. The moment my father decided to transfer the property, we found out the hard way that the stay order worked both ways, making distributing the estate difficult even for my father himself. Shortly after checking it off as a conquered hurtle on our list, it became a road block for us all over again. Furthermore, the official duplicates of the missing title documents would be needed to make the transfer. Avoiding intricate details, the CDA's procedures were lengthy, even though the duplicate was just going to its real owner. They first asked us to place newspaper ads into five newspapers in every major city in Pakistan saying that the original titles were stolen and if someone had any objection to issuing my father a duplicate, they should come forward immediately. The money for those ads had to come out of our own pockets, and they had to run for at least three days in each city. Then we had to wait a month before the CDA would move to the next step. The process was so needlessly complicated that it was still not completed by the time I returned to the US in June 2016.

CHAPTER 18

THROUGH THE WRINGER

This entire torturous affair had gotten my father thinking that he ought to have a will. Thus, in March of 2016 I was also making arrangements with Mr. Iqbal to bring my father to court for a will hearing in front of a judge, which is custom in Pakistan. It was not easy taking my father out of the house with his continuing prostate issue, though not impossible. Every time he walked through the police station or court house, urinary bag slung over his forearm, sloshing as he walked, stares followed him. The whole thing broke our hearts.

What is a statement of 164?

An official police statement, or biyan, taken after the occurrence of a crime typically carries no weight in Pakistani courts. Why? Because Pakistani police are known to be corrupt. The court system recognizes that police can coerce anyone into saying anything. When Pakistani police arrest someone and want to get information out of him or her, they can easily obtain a court order called a "remand". The dictionary defines the word remand as the act of placing a defendant on bail or in custody, especially when a trial is adjourned.

However, to remand someone in Pakistan means that the suspect is brought into custody and then brutally beaten by police until the suspect says something the police like. If police have a reasonable doubt about the truth of a suspect's statements and can point to evidence that suggests that a suspect is hiding information from them, obtaining a remand is as easy as asking a judge. Police remand scares the bejesus out of even the most dangerous criminals.

Perhaps the reasoning the judges use in handing over these remand orders is that the threat of legal police brutality can make the more dangerous criminals think twice before committing a crime, but whether this is right or wrong as a general practice in society still remains debatable in Pakistan. Now, it must be made clear that asking for a remand is not overly common for police, and they usually have some solid evidence against a suspect before they subject him to such treatment because a court must first approve the order.

Still, police are capable of anything during an investigation, and they are known to favor suspects who offer bribes and unduly punish others who offer nothing. Again this is not something set in stone and not all policemen are corrupt, but in Pakistani society, rightly or wrongly, police are generally perceived in this light. So if police cannot be fully trusted, who can be? The answer is the court system. Courts are still considered to be generally fair and, as an institution, not mired in corruption. The idea of bribing courts is still considered far-fetched and unheard of in Pakistan. (Thank heaven for that; otherwise, this country would be in chaos.)

Therefore, after recording a biyan with police, attorneys generally advise clients to record another biyan in front of a First Class Magistrate, who has powers equivalent to a judge. The idea is, if police have fudged anything during the investigation, such as favoring a particular party, at least you have a chance to straighten things out in front of a magistrate. But doing so is not a piece of cake. In an already overwhelmed system, allowing complainants to record these statements in court is often the last thing on a magistrate's mind. Thus, courts typically discourage this practice (though somewhat indirectly) for minor cases. Kidnapping, though, is anything but minor.

This statement recorded in front of a magistrate is called a "biyan of 164." Getting one for my father turned out to be a nightmarish ordeal, just as everything else had.

Due to resource constraints, magistrates are assigned a multitude of tasks, which are all deemed more important than recording citizens' statements all day long. For instance, most magistrates have field duties on an almost daily basis because they are responsible for enforcing laws for local businesses and communities. It seemed like whenever we went to the magistrate's office, their staff would tell us he or she was out in the field. To further complicate matters, their staff would have no idea when the magistrate would return to the office. For us that might mean sitting in magistrate's office waiting all day long, only to find out in the end he was not going to return back to the office that day. I wasted many days (to the tune of almost 2 weeks) trying to get this biyan recorded for my father.

Hello, can we have our "magistrate" please?

First of all, we were told we were required to go to the magistrate who had jurisdiction over my father's home address. His office was in sector F-8. When we went there in late March, we found out he was on vacation. When we asked if there was someone else covering for him, we were told to go to sector G-9, where many magistrates have offices. So the next day, my father had to leave the house again. He walked slowly across the parking lot, hauling the urine bag and visibly pained at every step. To make things worse, the Kohsar inspector was tagging along.

It was only 8 a.m., and we figured we would be the first ones to see the magistrate. Nope. The magistrate who was supposed to see our case was out of the office. We asked for some other magistrate and were told that the next one who would be able to help us was currently out in the field. When we asked when she was expected back in the office, the staff told us she would return "anytime now." We had no choice but to sit down and wait.

Luckily for us, the magistrate arrived after about half an hour, and she turned out to be a reasonably kind person. After seeing my father's condition, she immediately let us in. My father almost came to tears when he explained the situation to her, and she listened patiently and expressed sincere sympathy. I told her that I was visiting from the US to help my father, and we had a small chitchat about Donald Trump's chances of becoming the president. I got my hopes up that this meeting would turn out to be fruitful, but luck was still not on our side. When we told her why we were there, she pointed out a legal formality that had still not been met.

"The police should have recorded a biyan of 161 first," she said, smiling curtly at our "capable" inspector. He was caught pants down once again, sucking his thumb.

I have no idea what type of statement the police recorded in the hospital, but it wasn't a 161.

"The law also states that when a person first appears in front of a magistrate and tells his story verbally, the magistrate must give him twenty-four hours to think everything through before reappearing to record an official biyan of 164," said the magistrate. "I'm very sorry, but I can't help you today. Or any day. You'll need to return to the magistrate who has the proper jurisdiction over F-8. He should be back in his office tomorrow."

Our inspector said that he was "capable" enough to convince the magistrate that he could work on the 161 while the magistrate's staff took care of the 164, so first thing next morning, I took my father and the Kohsar inspector to the magistrate in F-8. Yet again, we were told that the magistrate was out in the field and that we needed to wait. He had not arrived by 1 p.m., and my father couldn't stay any longer. He was feeling sick and hungry, and because of his special diet, he had to eat at home. I asked him if he wanted to come back that day since the magistrate's office hours were till 4 p.m. He, however, wanted to call it a day. I was getting very worried that I wouldn't be able to accomplish much else before I had to return to the US.

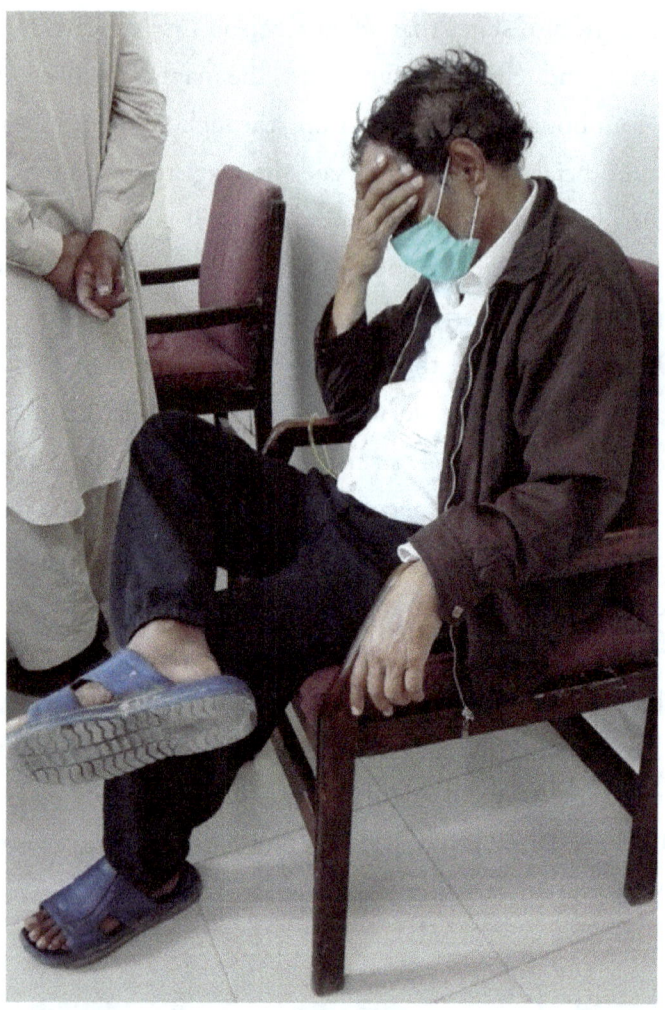

My father, sitting and waiting outside the magistrate's office. You can see the pipe for his urinary bag on the armrest of the chair. (Date: March 2016, Source: Author)

When we were given the same runaround the next day, stuck waiting for the absent magistrate from 8 a.m.–10 a.m., my father took the time to write him a letter. Fed up, I asked the Kohsar inspector if he could do something to expedite the meeting. Since policemen are always present during court proceedings, I thought he might know a fellow officer who could somehow help us out. Although he told me he would see what he could do, I had little confidence in him. I thought of a way to take action myself and approached the magistrate's special clerk, whom I had built a rapport with over our three visits.

"Is there any way you can help me get my father to see the magistrate faster?" I said, figuring a candid approach was best here. "He's in very poor health, and this back and forth travel and sitting here for hours at a time really isn't good for him."

To my amazement, the clerk leaned in conspiratorially and told me that the rest of the staff was lying to me; the magistrate was actually in a meeting two doors down, not out in the field. By the time I returned to where my father sat slumped in a hard chair, he was not only feeling sick but was also quite frustrated with how he was being treated. Not only was he a victim, he was a senior citizen trying to follow all the proper procedures laid out by Pakistani law, and yet he was being maltreated time and time again by authorities. When I told him that the magistrate was in the building and that his staff had been lying to us all along, he became downright furious.

He struggled to his feet and said, "I want to see him, wherever he is, right this moment!"

The clerk had already told me the room number, so we all walked down the hall and entered unannounced. My father's entrance was made less dramatic by his slow, pained, hampered walk. The inspector was a bit hesitant to interrupt the magistrate's alleged meeting, but he didn't really have a choice once my father and I barged in. Enough was enough.

When we entered the room, three people turned their heads our way. Our magistrate was sitting at a table with two other people who appeared to be fellow magistrates. Their "meeting" seemed more like a casual chit chat over coffee and tea to me. They seemed totally unconcerned, leaning back in their chairs, sipping on their cups, and having a good time. My father took the liberty of walking straight over to our magistrate and very respectfully explaining that he would like to talk to him. The magistrate, a clean-shaven man with thick black hair who appeared to be in his late forties, looked more than a little shocked at our blatant intrusion.

Not bothering to sit up in his chair, he asked coldly, "What do you need?"

In a deliberate but polite tone, my father quickly relayed his kidnapping story and requested to have a biyan of 164 recorded. I could tell from the magistrate's demeanor that he knew why my father was there. Surely his staff must have briefed him on my father's situation after we'd been talking to them for five days. We'd even sent him a note earlier that day.

> REQUEST FOR RECORDING OF STATEMENT OF 164
>
> DEAR ▮▮▮▮,
>
> IT IS SUBMITTED THAT I, SYED YUSUF MUBASHAR, SR (RTD) GOVT OFFICER AT PRESENTLY UNDER MEDICAL TREATMENT AND SERIOUSLY ILL CONSEQUENT UPON MY KIDNAPPING AND TORTURE. FOR THE LAST FIVE DAYS I AM TRYING MY LEVEL BEST TO RECORD MY STATEMENT OF 164 BUT STILL I HAVE NOT BEEN GIVEN THE CHANCE TO DO SO.
>
> MY HEALTH IS DETERIORATING DAY BY DAY AND INCASE I PASSED AWAY, DUE TO NOT HAVING RECORDED MY STATEMENT OF 164, THIS WILL HAVE A STRONG NEGATIVE BEARING ON THE CASE AND WILL CREATE NUMEROUS PROBLEMS FOR MY CHILDREN SO KINDLY, GIVE ME SOME TIME AT YOUR EARLIEST CONVENIENCE.
>
> THANKING YOU,
>
> MUBASHAR

A letter that my father wrote on the fly, with my assistance, while sitting inside the waiting room of the magistrate. (Date: March, 2016, Source: Author)

"A biyan of 164 isn't necessary for your case," he said. "That's only used as an extra layer of protection; it's nothing more than a formality."

My father and I gaped at each other for a moment. Mr. Iqbal had made it very clear that we *needed* this statement.

My father persisted, telling the magistrate that what had happened to him was serious business and that he wanted to protect himself from all angles. The magistrate didn't take kindly to being contradicted in front of his peers. He started arguing with my father, practically yelling at him, while my father cradled his urine bag and struggled to stand upright. The magistrate never asked him to sit.

"Look, I'm not going to get involved with this," the magistrate said. "It's not necessary. And if you get stuck in prolonged litigation with your opponents, my office will be dragged along with you in court!"

This was just unbelievable to me. If he was not there to serve citizens, what was the purpose of his job? Given the seriousness of the crime, shouldn't he be going out of his way to help my father rather than trying to avoid getting pulled into extra court proceedings? And he was complaining about all this to my ailing father without ever budging from his comfortable chair. Truth be told, I felt like punching him right in the face.

Our attorney comes to our aid

I stood there in complete awe of the magistrate's reaction. First of all, in Asian societies, it is a cultural norm that a younger person offer an elder person—let alone an elder person in such terrible shape—a chance to sit first. On top of that, this magistrate was arguing about something that was a required part of his job.

In the end, he gave us the wishy-washy response, "I will see what I can do for you," and asked us to leave and come back tomorrow at 1 p.m. The next day, we decided to get to the office around 11 a.m. to be safe and just sit and wait. I felt so sorry for my father having to go through all this, but there was little I could do.

Then I had the idea to call Mr. Iqbal and tell him about the whole situation. He immediately agreed to help and asked us to meet him at 11:30 in the court house, which was only a few blocks away. After greeting him, he asked me to follow him back down the street a few blocks to the office of another magistrate incidentally right next door to our magistrate. This magistrate was acquaintance of Mr. Iqbal. As soon as Mr. Iqbal entered, the magistrate got up from his seat and shook hands with him. They had a brief chit chat on how things were going before Mr. Iqbal brought my father's conundrum to the magistrate's attention and asked him if he could help in any way. Sure as God made little green apples, this magistrate was supposed to have a meeting shortly with *our* magistrate. When I called my father into the room, this magistrate was kind enough to offer my father a seat and actually had the decency to ask him how he was doing. I had a feeling we were onto something. Soon after, our magistrate entered the room, and he looked very surprised to see us waiting for him. Without saying anything to us, he sat down and started to talk with his buddy. After they had gotten comfortable, Mr. Iqbal casually slipped in a mention of my father's case and how important it was for him to record that biyan of 164.

To my utter disbelief, our magistrate started arguing with Mr. Iqbal about why this statement, although nice to have, was not an absolute necessity. I have deep respect for Mr. Iqbal, and not without reason; he did not attain the status of Supreme Court Advocate by chance. His years of experience and his calm demeanor brought me a sense of assurance that he was more than capable of handling this young magistrate, who was full of air and arrogance. When our magistrate was finished with his "nowhere does it say in the law" rant, Mr. Iqbal said something that almost caused me to jump out of my chair.

"You are absolutely right! It does not say anywhere in the law that recording this statement is a must."

I looked on, flabbergasted, until Mr. Iqbal raised a finger and said, "But, I have both a legal and moral obligation to protect my client. I think you and I both know a police statement is not always enough." He turned away from our brooding magistrate and instead addressed his friend. "I can't tell you how many times a statement to a magistrate protected my clients in court proceedings. One of my former students, who is now a First Class Magistrate, also, is always ready to serve citizens by providing this service. It may not be mandated by law, but it's the right thing to do. All of the magistrates I've ever known who remotely care about their duty are all eager to help people in this manner. Every student I have ever taught who has become a magistrate would be willing to do it all day long."

"He's absolutely right, you know," the friendly magistrate said, turning to our magistrate.

Clearly feeling the peer pressure, our magistrate caved in. "Okay, let's do this."

It only took him five days of putting a sick senior citizen through the wringer before he agreed. Before we could even celebrate, he told us we'd have to come back the next morning to record the statement because his calendar was already full with important meetings.

"And what if you're not in your office again?" I asked heatedly.

"In that case, I'll allow the biyan to be recorded without my presence."

I opened my mouth to ask why we couldn't just record it today while he attended his "important" meetings if it could be recorded in his absence, but Mr. Iqbal, seeing the anger in my face, shook his head to stop me.

"Please bring your father first thing tomorrow morning. It's very important," he said in a soothing voice.

Needless to say, I showed up with my father and the inspector in the magistrate's office once again bright and early the next morning. This time the magistrate's staff knew what to do and *finally* recorded my father's biyan of 164.

Thank God, or I'm not sure how the case against Sadaf Hassan Raza would have turned out.

CHAPTER 19

WHAT'S UP WITH THIS CAMOUFLAGE?

Now that we had the biyan of 164, the pressure on police was stronger than ever to make some arrests. Since they had no clue where Raza was, they put their heads together on how to get Riaz Khan.

Khan was expected to show up for the civil case he'd been granted by a judge, so it seemed like a no brainer to me to arrest Khan when he showed up for it. The Kohsar inspector gave us many assurances that police would do just that. Mr. Iqbal, however, had also dealt with this inspector enough to realize, as I had, that he was either extremely incompetent or very corrupt. So, during our meetings in the days prior to the court date, we worked on creating a fool proof plan that would prevent Khan from getting away. Our biggest concern was that Khan would get wind of the fact that he was being indicted for kidnapping and would be arrested during the court proceedings, and he would take advantage of Pakistan's allowance of bail before arrest, which is very easy to get, even for a kidnapper. This Pakistani custom is designed to save lawyers some time fighting for bail in open court. Everyone is entitled to bail, so if someone in Pakistan hears that the police have found reasonable cause to arrest him and plan to do so in the next few days, that person can appear before a judge preemptively to argue his case and petition for bail before an arrest is ever actually made. If Khan was granted this bail, the judge could not issue an arrest warrant because the "bail before arrest" basically skips that whole step. If Khan was not arrested, he would not be interrogated. He could also easily skip town. So, we wanted Khan and his attorney to be caught off-guard. We decided to wait to convince the judge to sign off on the arrest until Khan was already present, by laying out all the evidence right there in the court. The stress of worrying that Khan might get away was keeping me and my father up at night.

Mr. Iqbal warned that if Khan got away, it might take weeks if not months for another hearing, during which time his attorney might create a smoke screen to keep alluding arrest. I asked Mr. Iqbal to do whatever it took to keep this from happening. This meant preparing a strong case against Khan in the light of biyan of 164 and other existing evidence that brought Khan's prior misdeeds to light. We needed a "smoking gun" to get him arrested on the spot.

I started every day at 8 a.m. on the court steps and worked diligently with Mr. Iqbal, many times all day long, to gather evidence against Khan. The Kohsar inspector was still working on his biyan of 161, which the female magistrate in G-9 had made an issue of, so I gently pressured him to complete the report before the fast-approaching court date. I had to do whatever it took to get things done. If it meant picking up the inspector from the police station at 7 a.m. in the morning so that he was the first one in line at 8 a.m. when the court doors opened, I did it. If it meant picking up a file from somewhere personally, I did it. Sometimes it felt I was bending over backward and doing way more than I should have been, but I did not want any slip ups from anyone. Even Mr. Iqbal had me pick him up one day at 7:30 a.m. to be in court at 8 a.m. Quite frankly, I did this more than once, and even dropped him off at his residence on many occasions.

On one occasion, he told me that he'd forgotten a file he wanted at home, so I personally drove him to his house in the middle of day to pick up that file so that the task at hand would be finished the same day instead of being put off to the next. When my father found out how many times Mr. Iqbal had asked me for transportation, he balked at it and personally talked to Mr. Iqbal, telling him that this simply could not continue and that he must arrange his own transportation. I objected, warning my father not to upset Mr. Iqbal, but I guess he had a point; I, myself, had started to feel that I was being used. After my father had this conversation with our attorney, he eased up quite a bit on me.

But I don't regret my actions because I was making sure that all t's were crossed and all i's were dotted for the upcoming court hearing. I was determined to give every ounce of energy to help my father, and I will remain proud of this fact for the rest of my life.

Preparations for the court appearance

There was so much work involved in prepping for Khan's court appearance that Mr. Iqbal had called up two junior attorneys to assist him with gathering the evidence. The day before the court date, Mr. Iqbal worked with his junior attorneys until midnight at his home in order to finish everything in time. Overall, Mr. Iqbal did an excellent job, as usual. Being an Advocate of the Supreme Court, he was not the cheapest attorney, but whatever his fee, it was well worth it.

One day prior to the hearing, I also met with the inspector to make sure he had his ducks in a row. He still hadn't finished the biyan of 161, which was concerning to say the least. Mr. Iqbal had already hinted that he thought this inspector was not incompetent but, in actuality, corrupt. This made me extremely nervous. It meant that he might tip off Khan. However, there was nothing I could do to stop him apart from appealing to his ego. So, I tried to flatter him and gush about what a great job he was doing, hoping that would also speed up his progress. But in all fairness, I did not know if he would actually tip off Khan or not, and I kept my fingers crossed.

I used what little rapport I had already built with the Kohsar inspector to plead with him to complete the biyan of 161 before the court hearing the next morning and to be ready to make an arrest. He told me not to worry and assured me that police would be ready. Now, I don't know if it was my sixth sense or it had something to do with the way he was acting, the more he assured me not to worry, the more I worried. I had no option but to take his word for it. However, he did offer one favor in the form of a suggestion on how to protect myself in court the following day.

"Whether he's involved in the kidnapping or not, this Khan guy and his accomplices are criminals, and if they are looking to hurt your father, they're surely looking to harm you, too," he said. "You need to disguise yourself. Khan's gang members *will* show up, posing as casual observers of court proceedings, and you do not want them to recognize you as Mubashar's son, especially when you are a visitor from America. I suggest wearing a medical mask to hide your face.

They're allowed inside the court area as long as you aren't directly speaking with the judge."

I got his point and decided to wear a medical mask the next day, which was easy enough to obtain from Ali, who wore them regularly for his work. I decided to go the extra mile and also wore sunglasses and a hat.

A photo of me in a camouflage at the court house. I took this just minutes before appearing for the court hearing. The billboard behind me in Urdu reads, "Ijaz Law Associates." You can also see a lawyer (unknown) walking behind me. (Date: March 19, 2016, Source: Author)

I will get my day in court

On the designated court date, I took my father and Peter in our car and arrived at the court house a little before 8 a.m. I still had no way to recognize Khan, so I asked Peter to point him out when he appeared in court.

In Pakistan, multiple hearings are scheduled in the same court room each day, and the judge can only give so much time to each hearing. You go stand outside the court house and check the printed sheet already posted on the wall for your case number, and it will tell you the *approximate* time you will be called in. It is a good idea to get there half an hour early because if your name is called and you are not present, the judge will move your case to the end of the queue, meaning you may have to wait all day.

When we arrived outside the courtroom at about 7:45 a.m., fifteen minutes before it opened for the day, the corridors were slowly filling up with the usual hustle and bustle. We did not arrive together, exactly. On the way there, I had asked my father and Peter to go separate ways so that no one could tell I was Mubashar's son. So, we blended into the crowd, moving toward the court room from different directions. I kept an eye on Peter, watching for his signal that he had spotted Khan, hoping he would heed my instructions to *not* come calling my name. Looking around the growing sea of people outside the courtroom, I had no idea who was there for ordinary court business and who was there for malicious purposes. As I studied each face, I couldn't help but think about what Khan might do if he found out that I was working with police to orchestrate his arrest. He might already know; these criminals are smart. They also had the resources to find out who was instrumental in Khan's arrest after the fact. Either way, I had plenty of reason to think they would be gunning for me eventually. Suddenly, I was a little nervous about my disguise. I was the most peculiar looking character in the crowd. Who wears a medical mask, a hat, and sunglasses during a court hearing? Of course, I did not care if I was noticeable in general; I just did not want to be recognized as Mubashar's son.

The clerk started loudly calling names of the parties' right at 8 a.m. A look at the time sheet showed that the case of "Mubashar vs. Khan" was set for approximately 9 a.m. So, I just walked around the court area and sat down in a nearby office because many people were already giving me weird looks due to my camouflage. Around 8:45 a.m., I returned to the courtroom doors. I spotted the Kohsar inspector, who either did not recognize me or did not care that I was standing there in camouflage. I decided not to risk approaching him. I did see some sheets of paper in his hands but could not tell if it was the biyan of 161. Mr. Iqbal and I had prepared the case in such a way that even in the event the report was not ready, my father would do just fine in front of the judge.

I tried to peek inside and got a glimpse of the judge sitting at a table situated on a stage. Then, from the corner of my eye, I noticed Peter a few feet away, gesturing to me. It took a moment before the light bulb went on and I realized he was pointing to Khan. I followed Peter's finger and locked onto a man with a mustache. I asked Peter a question with my eyes, and he gave an affirmative nod. I was looking at the right guy. I stole a good look at Khan while he was engrossed in conversation with his attorneys, neither of which was the corrupt one we had been expecting. He was dressed in a traditional *shalwar kameez*, which is essentially a long, collared shirt that hits at the knees. Khan's was a pristine, plain white, and he wore pitch black, polished shoes. He was surprisingly well groomed. Besides his thick moustache, his face was clean shaven. He had pitch-black hair that was nicely combed. His calm demeanor, punctuality, and put-together appearance made me think he must not know anything about the upcoming arrest. Still, I couldn't be sure.

I snapped a photo of Riaz Khan on my cell phone without his knowledge. Unfortunately, I've been advised against publishing it here. Shortly after I put my phone away, the court clerk reappeared and called out, "All parties in Mubashar vs Khan should come inside now."

My heart was in my mouth, and I fought the urge to follow everyone inside right away. Instead, I hung back, not wanting to be seen as an active party member in this case. I watched as my father, Mr. Iqbal, his assisting junior attorney, the Kohsar inspector, Khan, and his two attorneys rushed in. I twiddled my thumbs patiently until everyone was situated and then casually took a seat in the back. I started to think my late entrance was a mistake because by the time I entered, I was the only one standing. Not exactly inconspicuous, but it didn't seem like anyone noticed. I really hoped not, because there were a lot of people in the room, and I had no way of knowing if some of them were Khan's accomplices.

After both attorneys introduced themselves to the court, there was some small talk between them and the judge that I could not hear. Two minutes later, everyone started filing outside again. Confused, I sat in my chair until my father and his two attorneys walked a good distance away from the courtroom. Unable to resist my curiosity, I approached them and asked what had happened.

"Khan's two attorneys told the judge that his real attorney is sick and could not show up on time," said my father. "He claims he'll be able to make it this afternoon, so the judge pushed us back until one."

There was nothing we could do except wait. I split off from my father as soon as I got the news. My father ate lunch with Mr. Iqbal, and I ate by myself at a spot within the court's vicinity. When one o'clock rolled around and my father was called in again, Khan's real attorney (corrupt) was present. Again, I found a seat in the back where I could inconspicuously make a little video of the proceeding.

What happened next made me want to cry into my camouflage!

Khan's attorney approached the bench and pulled out "bail before arrest" orders, which he'd obtained earlier from the court.

Someone had tipped Khan off about his upcoming arrest!

I just couldn't believe it, but I kept my composure during the court proceedings, which did not last for more than fifteen minutes. My father recounted his story of the kidnapping, but since Khan had already obtained bail before arrest, he could not be arrested that day. Court was adjourned that afternoon, and I came back home disheartened.

Later when I confronted our inspector as to who might have tipped off Khan, he said he had no idea. He told me the whole police department knew about my father's case and the plan to arrest Khan, so anyone could have used the situation to their advantage. To this day, I still don't know for sure who did this, but I am certain whoever it was, is definitely going to hell!

As I watched the inspector shrug his shoulders in a "tough luck" sort of way, something else started bothering me. It was the inspector who had asked me to wear a disguise, warning that Khan's accomplices would be present at the court hearing.

How in the world did he know that?

To this day I have my suspicions that it was the Kohsar inspector himself who tipped Khan off, obviously in exchange for some monetary gain. However, he never admitted it to me while I was in Pakistan.[15]

Thanks to whoever it was, Riaz Khan is still at large as of the December 2016 writing of this book.

---

[15] My father later told me in December 2016 that this inspector was indeed caught colluding with criminals and was forced to retire early due to his activities.

CHAPTER 20

THE TRICKSTER AMONG US

One Sunday afternoon in late March, growing tired of the daily grind of dealing with courts and police, I decided to go to a hill station near Islamabad called *Daman-e-Koh*. A hill station is a town built at a high elevation. The first hill stations were built by European colonists seeking refuge from the heat, and now they are used as tranquil getaways and hubs for fun. I decided to go on a Sunday so that it wouldn't be too busy in the middle of day. This is the same hill station my parents and I tried to reach on my father's first motorbike. My car made it to the top just fine that day, and I was walking around and enjoying the views of Islamabad when my phone started ringing. With my eyes still on the grand mountain ranges, Islamabad's lush green-belt, and the blue, sparkling waters of the Rawal lake, I answered. It was my father.

"Where are you?" my father asked in a wild voice. "You must come back home right away."

"Dad, what's wrong?"

"Just get back here, quick!"

Dropping everything at a moment's notice for some new urgent situation had sort of become a habit by then, so I rushed back to my car and started driving downhill toward home. I was careful to contain the gnawing panic so that my car didn't get away from me. My heart pounded all the way. As soon as I reached home, I saw Fiza already waiting for me on the front porch, bouncing her foot and wringing her hands. She rushed to me as I got out of the car.

"Fiza, what's wrong?"

"Dad just got a call… from Raza!"

"What?" I said, too loud to my own ears. "What did she say?"

"She said she was with her attorney, and she confessed to draining Dad's bank accounts and even luring him to the kidnapper's car, but she says her involvement stopped there. She had nothing to do with the actual planning of the kidnapping or anything that happened after she got him in the car."

"Are you serious?"

"Bhai, that's not all," said Fiza, eyes wide. "She told Dad who was really behind it all."

"Who?" I said, practically shouting now.

"Ghulam Yasir Abbas."

Despite the shock of having a definite answer, I can't say I was all that surprised to hear Abbas' name.

Dear Abbas, my father's newfound "best friend."

Fiza went on to explain that Abbas had been helped by his brother, according to Raza. Raza, herself, had made the revelation because she was upset that her name was all over the police reports while the real kidnapper's name was not mentioned anywhere. Most damaging of all, her name was all over the biyan of 164 we'd so painstakingly recorded with the magistrate, which was now on public record. My father could tell from the conversation with her that it did not bother her too much that her name was included in the police

FIR, but it definitely concerned her that the court statement named her as the prime suspect. She claimed she was not the mastermind at all but a mere accomplice. In a classic scenario, she had turned on her fellow criminals because she felt that she was getting more than her fair share of the heat. Now she wanted to make sure that the real masterminds got the appropriate punishment and that the majority of the blame was redirected off her. To prove her helpfulness, Raza later provided identification documents for everyone involved in the plot. According to her, it was Abbas' brother who had sat in the back seat next to my father, claiming that they were law enforcement and that my father was under arrest.

Ignoring red flags galore!

All my suspicions about this guy, Abbas, turned out to be true. My father had ignored numerous red flags about his renter from the very beginning. First, Abbas had not even flinched at the asking rent for the larger unit, even though Rs. 200,000 ($2,000 US) a month seemed very high to me by Pakistani standards. Stranger still was that he was a single man with a nominal job at the US Consulate, which only pays locally competitive salaries to the Pakistani citizens it employs. In order to afford a monthly rent of $2,000, Abbas would have to make something like $4,000 a month, which is exorbitant by Pakistani standards and would never be dished out by the consulate.

Also, recall that he told my father that he had gotten his name and info from the American Embassy website. Yes, my father is a prominent businessman in Islamabad, but I am not too sure that he is a man of such prominence that the American Embassy would mention his name on its website. Government agencies don't usually mention "preferred landlords" on their website anyway, because it would cause an outcry among local businessmen about favoritism.

My father also completely ignored the fact that the US Consulate houses almost all employees inside the four walls of its compound or at least in sector F-5 (the Diplomatic Enclave), where it is located. Due to security concerns, the US Government bars its employees from living outside F-5 on their own. All diplomats who live in or need access to the Diplomatic Enclave are issued special ID cards, which are scanned at the entry gates. My father didn't ask to see this card. He didn't even seem to think it odd that a consulate employee would want to live all the way out in F-7. Any employee important enough to afford the apartment's rent would have been heavily encouraged to live within the Diplomatic Enclave. Since Abbas was living alone, it should have been required.

My father later told Fiza, Ali, and I that Abbas was always trying to show off and that he appeared very rich. He would often arrive in luxury vehicles (that we later found out were rented) and always talked big. There was no way his wages as a Pakistani citizen would allow him to afford Mercedes and Land Cruisers.

What was truly mind boggling was that my father did not conduct any sort of background check. He didn't even confirm Abbas' employment with the US Consulate. Whenever I had asked or tried to confront him about Abbas, he had always brushed me off, unwilling to listen to anything negative about him. That was how well Abbas had charmed him.

Abbas did not gain my father's trust overnight though. They met regularly for months, often at my father's residence, before any serious deals were stuck. Abbas had asked my father to form a joint venture with him to bring the first Starbucks to Pakistan, appealing to my father's adventurous business side. Abbas told my father that Starbucks was actively looking for franchisees in Islamabad. The fact of the matter is that Starbucks doesn't have a single franchised coffee shop anywhere in the world as of this writing in late 2016. All coffee shops operated by Starbucks are company owned. A small amount of due diligence on my father's part regarding Abbas' proposals would have brought his chicanery to light.

In general, the most glaring sign of trouble for me is when someone goes out of their way to impress me. This holds true whether it's business dealings, job interviews, or even trying to get a date. It's true everybody tries to look their best; however, after a few meetings, I should have a good idea of where they stand—whether it be a business or personal relationship—and I expect them to stop unnecessarily trying to impress me. If I get the feeling a person isn't showing me their true self, I immediately start to get nervous. But that's just me.

Abbas never ceased making self-proclamations of his wealth and expanded business interests. He made it clear to my father that making rent payments of $2,000 per month was not an issue. I think my father was schmoozed by these lofty claims. He must have been rather impressed if not outright intimidated by Abbas' acts of extravagance in such a poor country. This showed in his willingness to discuss a business partnership and in inculcating tales of Abbas' business acumen in me. My father's personal explanation for the lack of due diligence, however, was simply that his property had been sitting vacant for too long, and he just wanted it rented out. As the saying goes, haste makes waste.

As much as it pains me to say it, Abbas was an exceptional

con artist. After his guilt was confirmed, I found myself thinking, time and again, back to the phone call my father had with Abbas in Shahpur. My father had cried to and sought comfort from the man who had orchestrated all the atrocities committed against him. Ali, too, had witnessed numerous heartfelt phone calls between my father and Abbas while he was in the hospital. In one instance, my father had asked Ali to leave the room to take a call from Abbas in absolute privacy to which Ali took some offence. On many of those calls, Abbas told my father he was calling from the US on important assignments. However, the police verified that it was all lies. He obtained a US phone number through Skype, so when he dialed via Skype, the US number would appear, and it was always NY area code. Abbas never worked for the US Embassy, and he never left Pakistan. Abbas had truly blinded and cajoled my father to the extreme.

Sometimes I wonder, if Raza had never told us that Abbas was behind the kidnapping, would my father never have found out the truth? My father had proven his naïvety in regards to everything involving Abbas, so it's possible he would have continued to fraternize with his kidnapper indefinitely. A scary thought!

Was our cook involved also?

One thing that had continued to puzzle me was why my father's cook, Nina, showed up for work on her day off that Thursday when our house was burglarized. Fiza and I worried she might have been involved.

The police questioned her and confiscated her cell phone to see if she was ever in touch with the kidnappers. However, she was cleared when they could not link any phone call made or received to Abbas, Raza, or anyone else suspicious. It also didn't make much sense that she would have showed up at the house on the planned day of the burglary and called Fiza to alert her to the fact that no one was around and the doors were locked if she was indeed an accomplice.

My father had his own conversation with Nina, and she assured him to his face that she had nothing to do with his kidnapping. Her explanation for showing up on her day off was that she had taken that Monday off, and she wanted to compensate for it by working that Thursday. Her story made complete sense, and my father kept her in his employ.

Mistake Du Jour

It was shocking to realize that my father had not only been giving his kidnapper all the information about his health, but also providing him with intricate details of law enforcement's progress and suspects. It still floors me that my father, a smart businessman, was so bluntly fooled by a con man. The whole thing seems ludicrous, but in reality, smart people fall prey to con artists all over the world all the time.

As for Abbas, I must admit that all the alarm bells that had ever sounded in my head were due solely to strange occurrences and actions on his part, not due to any conversation with him. He was very soft spoken and compassionate, and his demeanor would not have raised an iota of suspicion. So, I suppose I understand how my father was never suspicious of him himself, especially since Abbas fixed his charms on my father harder than anyone else. I have never met Abbas in person, and I hope I never do. Although, I admit, I am slightly curious to lay eyes on the man who was bold and capable enough to carry out such a hideous plan. It's hard to believe anyone can be so cold and calculating as to befriend an aging man as the crux of a plot to steal his life's work, torturing him in the process, and then plan to kill him and make it look like a car accident to wrap everything up in a neat bow. Had the final part of the plan worked, he would have gotten away with it. The sophisticated forensic technologies of the West are not yet available in Pakistan, and it would have been difficult for detectives to discover the drugs in my father's system and distinguish his torture injuries from injuries obtained in a car accident. The only forensic evidence that would have been concrete were the fingerprints on the stamp papers obtained from my father at gun point. My siblings and I would have lost our father and been left with nothing, without anything to prove these criminals wrong.

I can't speak for Fiza and Ijaz, but had Abbas and his accomplices succeeded in their plot, it would have been almost impossible for me to crawl out of that emotional black hole. I don't intend to preach, but I firmly believe in my heart that my father's survival was an act of God. My father had earned his estate fairly in the eyes of God through hard labor, and he has every right to enjoy it while he lives. It belongs to no one else.

Well, obviously we called police right away about Sadaf's claims. Police naturally informed her attorney that she needed to be questioned in person, but her attorney started making excuses and asked that she be questioned over the phone only. Police conducted a few phone interviews with Raza, but I am not privy to any information regarding whether or not they traced her location during those calls, as I would hope they did.

During those calls, Raza claimed her son was kidnapped by Abbas and his men and that they threatened to harm her son should she refuse to act as an accomplice in looting Mubashar's accounts.

What an absolute absurdity!

During those days, my father had asked me to work only on civil matters such as dealing with the CDA, so I am not well-informed on how aggressively police pursued Raza. She was also purportedly a UK citizen, and at times, police told my father she had fled the country. At one point, police said she was in the UK and at another occasion she was allegedly in Dubai. Obviously my father was taking police's word for it, and there was no way for him to confirm the validity of the information. The lack of zeal that police had shown toward apprehending Raza thus far had been mind boggling, and it hasn't improved. She had not been apprehended when I returned to the US in June 2016.[16]

After gaining this information about real the masterminds of the kidnapping from Raza in late March 2016, I also asked police to up the ante for apprehending Abbas. At least according to police, Abbas had a US Visa, and he was thinking about fleeing to the US. However, some detective work done by police later on uncovered that one of Abbas' brothers had a court date (the whole family seems to be criminals) in the city of Sargodha, and Islamabad police wanted to go there for more investigation. In rare circumstances, police can apprehend a sibling (especially one with a criminal record) and use him as collateral to get the suspect they are after. However, the Kohsar inspector went to two separate court dates in that remote town about four hours away from Islamabad and came up empty handed both

---

[16] Toward the end of 2016, police did add Sadaf Hassan Raza into a "wanted" list of criminals, which is published in the newspaper.

times. In one instance, he told us that no one showed up at the court hearing. In the second instance, his excuse was that the criminals must have gotten wind of the attempted arrest, because they sent a relative to obtain a new court date. There was no way for my father to corroborate these statements made by this Kohsar inspector.

Another dimension of Abbas' cleverness was revealed when we realized, his name had never been officially recorded anywhere! Not in any police FIR, not in the biyan of 164, nowhere whatsoever. At the time all of those were recorded in early to mid-March, Abbas had still been considered a family friend beyond suspicion. Although this should not keep authorities from arresting him, my father never suspecting him has helped him a great deal.

After Raza confessed to taking part in the kidnapping plot and revealed the names of the masterminds, my father felt quite relieved that now he knew the identities of all his enemies who had ever wanted to harm him. All police had to do now was find them.

Or so he thought!

CHAPTER 21

MUDDLED MOTIVES

As soon as my father began to feel better toward the end of March (right after we discovered Abbas' guilt), we got back in touch with Khalid, the Norwegian national who wanted to rent the back portion of the house. Now that my father was in a little better shape both physically and mentally, he wanted to finalize the finer details of the lease contract and get that space filled.

Inviting Khalid back to sign the final contract

When I called, we arranged a meeting between six and seven that night, after Khalid finished up at work. As we talked, I peeked out the window at the fully armed guard posted outside. We still hadn't told Khalid anything about the kidnapping, but I was concerned the 24/7 security alone might spook him. I told him goodbye with a tight knot in my throat and hoped he did not probe me too much about the reason behind our sudden boost in security. My father needed this lease to go through.

A little after 6 p.m., I started sneaking peeks out the window. On the third pass, I saw him. Khalid stood frozen, sweat shining on his chubby face, his mouth hanging slightly open as he stared at our security guard, who simply stared back with a stoic expression. I leaned my head out the window and nodded to the security guard to let him in. Khalid rushed toward the house, and I came to meet him under the car porch. The large man panted a little as he threw a finger over his shoulder at the rifle-wielding guard and said, "That guy is terrifying!"

I tried not to show my surprise. "Why? He's a security guard. He keeps people safe."

"I... I just don't like armed men."

My puzzlement grew. I had expected him to ask a lot of questions about why we had decided on security all of a sudden, but I hadn't expected him to be scared of the guards. Despite having some questions, he should have been pleased that he would basically get top dollar security for free, as many foreigners routinely hire security companies on their own dime in Islamabad. The oddest thing of all, though, was that, as the alleged Chief of Narcotics for the Norwegian government in Pakistan, he should have been more than comfortable with security companies, law enforcement, and armed men in general.

I have always prided myself on my instincts. I truly believe that instinct is a special gift from God, derived from thousands of years of evolution when humans were animals relying solely upon their instincts to survive, and people who ignore their gut feelings do themselves a great disservice. I know that whenever I have ignored my instincts, I incurred a loss in one way or another.

In that moment, standing under the car porch with Khalid, everything inside me was screaming that something was amiss.

"Well, there's no need to worry about those guys. I'm sure you see plenty like them in your line of work, don't you?"

"Yes, well…"

"Your job seems very exciting. What all do you do on a day-to-day basis?"

I kept the direction of the conversation focused on him and his duties, and he opened up pretty quick. Soon he was bragging about how easy it was for him to make money in his profession.

"The drugs and money seized by the task force are often… unaccounted for, if you know what I mean. Plus these dealers are always ready to bribe their way out of trouble."

I asked him why he felt the need to engage in illegal activity to make more money if his government was giving him a handsome enough salary to approve his application for a place with a rent of $5,000.

"Look, I'm fifty-five years old. If I make as much money as I possibly can right now, I can retire comfortably in fifteen years. My profession allows me to make some extra money on the side, so why not make it happen?"

Ali came out the door, getting ready to hop in his car and go home. He looked at us curiously as he passed. I talked lower as I watched him go. Inside my head, alarm bells and sirens blared, but I did my best to adopt a "Why should I care?" attitude on the outside.

"Khalid, are you doing this just to make more money, or do you have some other motive?"

"Making the maximum amount of money I can in my lifetime is my only motive."

My phone rang. Khalid leaned his head closer as I pulled the phone from my pocket.

"Someone from the USA," he said matter-of-factly.

It was my wife. I talked just long enough to tell her I had to call her back. I was surprised by how aware Khalid was of his surroundings. He asked me briefly what kind of work I did in the US and how many children I had.

As I walked inside after saying goodbye to Khalid, I considered stopping the whole thing and telling my father that his new tenant was dishonest and corrupt, but decided against it. I did not want to burden him with more negativity, and I figured Khalid's misdeeds toward his government had little to do with my father, so long as Khalid paid his rent checks on time. Still, our chat under the car porch had instilled me with a feeling of slight unease.

I don't want to blow my secret

Toward the end of March, the lease still hadn't formally been signed, and Khalid was becoming more and more impatient. He texted or called me almost every day, trying to gauge if my father's condition was stable enough for him to finalize the agreement and move into the house as soon as possible. He was sick of the temporary accommodation provided by the Norwegian Embassy. He never did find out about my father's kidnapping, for which I was grateful.

When Khalid called and told me the check for the first year's rent had arrived from Norway, already payable to the landlord, I saw no reason whatsoever to delay the process any further since my father was finally feeling better. I invited Khalid over right away to get the lease signed. However, as it turned out, it would take more than one meeting to come to an agreement on the details like who would pay for electricity, gas, water, etc.

Because legal agreements in Pakistan need to be on stamp paper, every time there was a change in the written lease, it had to be reprinted. Stamp paper is only sold by licensed vendors and is not readily available at all times. More often than not, you end up in a courthouse to make the purchase, which isn't cheap. Thus it becomes a serious pain if you're in a hurry and have to make too many amendments to the agreement. It didn't help that Khalid was requesting the lease agreement be made out in his wife's name, Naila Sharif. Whenever my father put his signature on any draft of the contract, Khalid always had to bring it back home with him to get his wife's signatures. This seemed odd to me, and I asked him why he wanted it done that way. He said that since he was a "secret" agent of the Norwegian government, he did not want his identity on a public document. My father didn't have any objections to this, so I did not make a big issue out of it. Furthermore, the lease negotiations were already underway before my involvement, with at least one draft already signed in Khalid's wife's name, so I stayed out of it. I did, however, make sure to ask my father if he had obtained all of Naila Sharif's identification documents, and he said he had. However, when I asked him to show them to me, he could not remember where he had placed them.

During one of our meetings, I asked Khalid to provide us with a copy of his identification as well his wife's, just for verification purposes.

"I don't want to blow my secret cover by revealing my identity to you," he said.

Again this struck me as odd. It was not as if we were going to tell the whole world that he was an undercover agent of the Norwegian government; we just wanted to verify who he was, in fact, a government employee.

"The whole reason I've gone to all the trouble of having the lease signed in my wife's name is to keep my identity secret," he said. "I don't want to reveal my identity to anyone, even if it means walking away from this lease."

I softened my stance a little after seeing his stubbornness. It wasn't my call, and my father had already agreed to sign the lease with Khalid's wife's name and IDs only. I backed off and only insisted upon new copies of his wife's identification. He did not argue once I explained that my father had misplaced the previous copy. Having become somewhat paranoid by the time he handed over his wife's Norwegian passport, I made several hard copies and also scanned it to my computer for my own records.

Throughout all the negotiations, I never met Naila in person. This wasn't too unusual; Pakistan is a conservative country where women are not expected to get involved in business affairs too much. My father told me he had met Naila when the couple came for the first showing of the house. My father's office secretary, Noor, had also met the couple that day. My father said Noor was perfectly comfortable with the couple, but Noor herself later confessed to me this was not at all true.

Crack open the champagne, and let's get the party started

We finally sat down and signed the agreement on April Fool's Day. To my surprise, Khalid brought a stamp paper vendor along with him to the signing. The idea was simple; if there was still any error or amendment to be made, a new stamp paper could be furnished right away. He was eager to get it all done that day.

This lease agreement clearly stipulated that my father would receive a sum of $60,000 as advance rent for the first year of occupancy. After the first year, Khalid (technically his wife) reserved the right to extend his agreement for another year, and the monthly rent could be renegotiated.

Everything was signed and then Khalid left with the keys to his portion of the house. He said his goodbyes at the door but turned back as he approached the gate. He said he was having a get together at his house with some of his friends that coming Sunday, and he invited my father and me to come if we liked.

I cupped my hand at the side of my mouth and shouted down the drive, "When should we be there?"

"Oh, I will call you and let you know later."

My father and I sat down in the living area, happy that negotiations had gone well. As far as we knew, Dad had a solid tenant and would soon receive a handsome sum of $60,000. I suppose I should have known the universe would play a joke on April Fool's Day.

CHAPTER 22

INVADERS

The next day, Saturday, was relatively calm, and I went to a shopping district in Islamabad called Karachi Company. This huge marketplace occupies an area of about one square mile, and you can buy anything imaginable there, from clothes to furniture to refrigerators. I went to buy gifts for my children and wife, and to get my mind off of the daily grind of dealing with police and the courts. It was fun to people-watch in the crowded marketplace. The day ended quietly, and that evening, I helped my father draft letters to high-ranking officials, such as the Chief of the Army Staff, the Inspector General of Police, the Interior Minister of Pakistan, and a few others. Now that we had more concrete details about the guilty parties, the idea was to get the word out about this kidnapping to as many people as possible so that we could seek additional help rather than just relying on the meager efforts of police.

Calm before the storm?

On Sunday morning, I enjoyed the day in another marketplace called the Sunday Bazaar, which is a make-shift market assembled by vendors only on Sundays. Everything is removed by Sunday evening. I am an extremely frugal guy—a skill inculcated in us by our father in early childhood—so I always enjoy going to markets where I can find good bargains. My parents always used to go to this Sunday market when my mother was alive, mostly to buy fruits and vegetables, although you can buy other household items like clothing, shoes, and decorative items, too. These markets are typically crowded with a lot of hustle and bustle, and you can see people from many walks of life. Interestingly, I have known a lot of wealthy people in Islamabad who go to the Sunday Bazaar, although they don't have any financial need to do so.

When I came back home that evening, I asked my father if he planned to go Khalid's dinner party. He told me he did, but for some reason he asked me not to join. He said that I was a visitor from the US and must keep a low profile. Why he said that still doesn't make much sense to me even today. The main reason I wanted to join was that I had developed a good rapport with Khalid during the negotiations, and I had the inclination to meet with his other colleagues. I did not have the heart or energy to argue with my father, though, so I obeyed his wishes.

I am a true believer that God does for you what's in your best interest. I have always lived my life with this belief. Even when an incident seems like a misfortune at the time, I try to find God's meaning behind it. Now this is easier said than done. It's also easier to believe and agree with when you have a good fortune but a little harder when a misfortune strikes. So I have made it a point in life to not only believe in God but also to *believe God*. This calls for a true belief that God looks out for what is in your best interest more often than not. And that sometimes means not crying foul when things go wrong and instead trying to find hidden meaning behind disaster. As it turned out, not going to Khalid's party would turn out to be a blessing in disguise.

While my father went to the party, I decided to go to the nearby Centaurus Mall. Thanks to load-shedding, power in F-7 goes out from 8 p.m. to 9 p.m. every day. I could either get out of the house or sit out that hour in complete darkness. Centaurus Mall has its own generators, so power never goes out there, and stopping by at night had become a habit during my four-month stay in Islamabad. The mall has four floors with a lot of shopping options, and the food court is a nice place to enjoy dinner.

I must have reached the mall around 7:30 p.m. and just hung around among the lively Sunday crowd. Centaurus is a rather high-end mall by Pakistani standards, and numerous American and European name brands have a presence there. Dolce & Gabbana, Gucci, Nine West, and Bonanza stand side by side with popular Pakistani brands like Caanchi & Lugari and Gul Ahmad. As for eateries, there are things like McDonald's, KFC, Hardy's, Mr. Cod, and Second Cup.

What's the commotion?

I ordered some food and settled down in the food court to eat. I was almost done with my meal when my phone rang. It was my wife. I had just started updating her on how things were going when a beep in my ear told me Ali was calling. I tapped the "ignore" option on my phone, thinking I would just call him shortly. Only seconds later, the insistent beep sounded in my ear again. It was Ali. Something was up. I told my wife I'd have to call her back later and switched over to Ali's call.

I had hardly said hello before he was screaming in my ear.

"Where are you?"

"Centaurus Mall."

"Come back home right now!"

"Why? What's going on?"

"Men with guns just broke into Mubashar's house!"

I almost dropped my phone. I sprinted across the mall to the elevators. I fidgeted impatiently, tapping at the button, willing the doors to open. When they finally did, I rushed inside the crowded space, shoving people aside to make room.

"Sorry, emergency," I said when they gave me nasty looks. Some stepped aside for me when the elevator opened at the underground garage. Once inside the car, I whipped out of the garage and got onto the main road in less than a minute. Only five more to go.

One hand on the wheel, I called Ali.

"Where are you?" I asked.

"I'm standing right outside. I called the Islamabad Police and the PIMS Police."

"How did you find out they were in the house?"

"Fiza called me. She was here when it happened."

"Where is she? Is she still in there?"

"No, she escaped with the baby and called from a neighbor's house."

"Is she okay?"

"Yes, yes, thank goodness."

"Have you talked to Dad?"

"I've been calling him this whole time, but his phone is off."

I swerved around slow-moving cars, barely avoiding an accident, cutting people off and veering in and out of lanes. I hardly cared. My goal was to reach home as fast as possible. As I approached the neighborhood, my first thought was to find my sister and nephew before anything else, but I had no idea which house Fiza had called from. I thought I would just drive around and try to find her in the streets. So I first drove by our house where I saw a single police vehicle sitting outside with its lights flashing and then drove up and down the nearby streets. But I didn't find her. I called her as I drove, but it just kept ringing. I also tried my father's phone, but it didn't even ring; it was powered off.

In a sudden flash of thought, I called the cell phone vendor who had helped us wrangle that First Information Report out of the Islamabad Police so we could get my father out of Shahpur. He was so well connected with the Kohsar police department, I figured he could help me get more officers to the scene. To my relief, he picked up. He was shocked to hear that armed intruders had entered our house, and he assured me he would make sure more officers were dispatched.

I was operating purely on instinct now, doing anything that my gut told me to do. As I drove around the streets, I wondered how anyone had gotten past our rifle-wielding security guard. Had there been a gun battle on the front lawn? Where was the security guard now? I lapped by the house again and saw the same police car still parked at the front gate with its lights on but no siren. I knew Ali was there dealing with police, so I continued my search for Fiza. I wrapped around the back street one more time and stomped on the breaks. Fiza was standing out in front of a house with her child in her arms.

I motioned to her to get inside. The street was dark, with only one streetlamp lit in the distance. She squinted in my direction, looking scared. She hesitated. I waved again, and she recognized me. As soon as she'd gotten in, I asked her to tell me what had happened.

"Bhai, it was Khalid!" she said. "I was just sitting there, waiting for Dad to get back from the party, and Khalid burst in with two other guys and two women. The men all had guns. They started shouting, 'Khalid owns this house now. Everyone else needs to get out. If you don't, we start shooting.'"

"What?" I shouted, dumbfounded. "Khalid?"

"Yes."

"What did you do?"

"The two women came up to me, and one of them slapped me in the face and demanded to know who I was. I was so scared and confused, but I knew I didn't want them to know who I was, so I said I was just a visitor. None of them seemed to recognize me, and I think it worked. The women took my phone, purse, and laptop."

"How did you get out?"

"While they were all distracted trashing the house, I snuck right out the front. They saw me when I opened the door. I had the baby in my arms, and when the two women tried to grab me, I didn't think I'd be able to beat them off. I just kept running, and the back of my shirt tore, and I got loose. I started running toward the security guard at the gate, screaming my head off for him to help me, but he just turned his back on me and told me to get back inside the house and be quiet."

I simply could not believe what I was hearing.

Dad is missing... again

I headed for PIMS to drop Fiza off safely at home.

"Where's Dad, do you know?" Fiza asked.

"I don't know. Last I saw him, he was heading to Khalid's party. If he wasn't with you in the house, and he wasn't with Khalid and his buddies when they attacked you, then I have no idea. His phone is off."

"So you think Khalid did something?"

"That's what it looks like." I groaned. "I can't believe any of this. Could you pinch me? I'm really hoping this is a dream."

She gave a blank look.

When I dropped her at her house, I told her not to open the door for anyone except me or Ali. I told her I'd call on her home phone if I needed anything, since her cell had been taken.

As I drove back home, I called one of my brother's friends whom I'd met while my father was still at the hospital. I told him I was going to ask for a favor right now that he could not refuse. I asked him to take an army of friends and drive straight to our house. He asked me what happened, and I briefly told him about the invasion, telling him I needed serious manpower. He said he would be there soon with a few more friends. I was on our street when the Kohsar Station House Officer (SHO), the equivalent to a sheriff, called me.

"Where are you?" he asked.

"Standing right in front of my house."

"Come into the station when you're done there."

"Be there in a few minutes."

Before rushing to the police station, I thought that I ought to make a round inside our house. When I entered through the front gate of our house, the security guard was still just standing there with a gun. There were a couple of police officers under the front car porch, and through the large front window, I saw two ladies standing inside our house and peeking out onto the porch. The thinner one had long hair and an elongated face. The other was traditionally dressed in shalwar-kameez and had a head scarf covering her hair. She had a round, chubby face. Both appeared to be in their late thirties or early forties.

Ali came out of the house arguing with some officers.

"You can't just let those women walk out of here," he said, anger tightening his jaw. "They've just helped commit a home invasion. They need to be arrested and punished!"

I called Ali to me and told him I had dropped Fiza and the baby off at home, safe and sound. We talked briefly about what Fiza had told each of us, piecing the whole thing together as best we could. The security guard was standing off to the side, and when I caught sight of him out of the corner of my eye, I rounded on him.

"Why didn't you do anything?" I said, jabbing a finger at him. "Isn't that what we pay you for?"

"There were too many men for me to handle alone," he said.

"Oh, really?" My eyes found Khalid's vehicle, parked neatly under the car porch. "How'd he even get in here? You just unlocked the gate and let armed men roll right inside? Did you even call the police?"

"No," he said, tone even and unapologetic.[17]

I couldn't speak I was so dumbfounded by this response.

---

[17] We obviously fired this sleazy security guard. We also made sure his employers were aware of his conduct, and we filed an official complaint against him with police.

Later, some day laborers working near the house told me that they had witnessed Khalid bribing this security guard.

This was all so crazy; I knew I needed to go speak with the SHO, fast. I told Ali to stay put and keep police from releasing those two women while I went to the station to sort all this out. Before I left, though, I asked him if he knew where my father was. He still had no idea. He had no clue where Khalid or his male accomplices were either. They appeared to have run off before anyone arrived. I gave my father's cell one more try, and it was still off. I was becoming very nervous.

When I arrived at the police station, I went straight to the SHO's office. He greeted me and asked me to sit down. A senior inspector sat next to him. When the SHO saw the panicked look on my face, he asked me to calm down.

"It appears that some people have tried to seize your father's house under the claim that he obtained a loan for Rs. 60,000,000 ($600,000 US) from one of these men and put his house up as collateral," he said. "They claim he has failed to pay it back, so the house is now the claimant's."

"And just who is this claimant?"

"His name is Khalid—"

"Wow!" I said, shaking my head in utter disbelief. "Where is Khalid now?"

"In police custody. He's locked up in one of our cells."

I breathed a little easier. The SHO had not fully bought Khalid's story, at least not yet.

"Do you know this guy?"

"Of course I know the guy," I said. "He just signed a lease to rent out the back portion of my father's house. There's no loan or any sort of collateral agreement. Never was."

The SHO asked me to go with the inspector and talk to Khalid in lockup. The cell was in a building right next door. Inside, only one light bulb dimly illuminated the concrete floor and the man sleeping on a bed just behind Khalid, who stood at the bars. It smelled of rust and unwashed men. When he saw me, Khalid started shouting curses at me in perfect Urdu. I approached the cell, shocked, and when I got close, he shoved his arms through the bars and tried to grab me and slam me into his cell. The inspector ordered him to back off, and asked me to step away. As I backed off, Khalid kept angrily cursing at me.

"Come on," said the inspector. "We aren't getting anywhere here. Please follow me back up to the office."

When we were back in the office, the SHO asked us what had happened. His inspector explained that Khalid had said nothing but curses and had tried to assault me. A look at the clock told me it was close to 10 p.m., and worry for my father consumed me once again. I asked the SHO if he knew anything about his whereabouts.

"Sorry, I don't know anything yet, but my men are searching for him."

"Sir, as you know, he's a kidnapping victim. He has enemies, and he still isn't completely well. We need to find him!"

The SHO assured me he understood the gravity of the situation and that finding my father was the police's first priority.

I mentioned Khalid's invitation to my father, hoping that would somehow help.

Had Khalid done something to my father?

Corrupt attorneys to the criminal's aid

As I was relaying my suspicions that Khalid and his accomplices might have harmed my father, three people entered the room unannounced. As they moved to sit down, I recognized one of them. It was none other than Khan's corrupt attorney!

I fixed him with a cold, angry stare full of hatred and disgust. Recognition lit his eyes, and he returned the favor. As our eyes locked onto each other for a few tense seconds, I wanted nothing more than to leap from my chair and beat the shit of out him. However, the other two men either did not realize who I was or did not care about my presence. They just started up a conversation with the SHO, never apologizing for interrupting. From the conversation, it was easy to tell both of them were attorneys. This trio of attorneys launched into a prepared story, saying that there was indeed an agreement between Khalid and Mubashar in which Mubashar had obtained a loan of Rs. 60,000,000. Because Mubashar had failed to repay him, Khalid was entitled to seize and occupy the property. Then they presented this agreement to the SHO, laying it in front of him on his table.

I sat there speechless, in absolute awe at their boldness. It was obvious to me that this gang of criminals had carefully selected the best crooked attorneys to game the system in their favor, but I held my tongue and listened. They claimed that because Khalid had a right to seize the property by virtue of this loan agreement (fabricated); this was all a civil case and not a police matter at all. They argued that just as a bank seizes property for non-payment of a loan, their client was entitled to do the same. Thus, Khalid was no criminal and must be let go. They also said that Khalid would continue to occupy the property until a court reached a decision.

I can honestly say I have never felt that scared in my entire life.

If these corrupt attorneys could convince the SHO that this was not a police matter, but a civil contract dispute case, the SHO would have no right to hold their client in lockup. If the SHO let Khalid go that night, by their argument, that meant he would be free to go back to our house and occupy it until courts decided whether the agreement was a sham.

Yeah, right, good luck with that!

It could literally take the courts years to come to a decision and order Khalid to vacate the premises. And all that time, this scoundrel could freely occupy our house. The toll that a fight for our own house would take on our family was unimaginable. God only knew what other schemes they would come up with to tie us up in courts even longer. In the end, my father would doubtless lose his estate and his children's inheritance—the same house he had built with great efforts and where all us siblings grew up.

Just thinking about it sent chills down my spine. My mind raced to find a solution as I watched the attorney's work. They certainly meant business. So much so, one of them had actually brought a law book with him, and he opened it to a specific page, put it in front of the SHO, and pointed to a section of the law that he said proved his client was entitled to the property. I was just thunderstruck by the lengths these attorneys were going to help a criminal deprive honest people of their estate. My mother had always taught me to seek God during times of great distress. I said a deep, silent prayer.

"Please, God, let this SHO be a strong man and not succumb to these crooked men!"

CHAPTER 23

GO GET 'EM

Once the SHO had listened to what the attorneys had to say, he asked them to leave the room. However, he did not ask me to leave. Maybe God was listening. As soon as the trio left the room, I could not help jump out of my chair to get closer to the table where this alleged loan agreement was still sitting in front of the SHO. It looked like the lease agreement my father and Khalid had signed in our home, but it was backdated a few months. The SHO placed his finger on a specific clause and asked me to read it.

Instead of stipulating that my father would receive a sum of Rs. 6,000,000 as the first year's rent, this lease agreement had been altered somehow to read that my father had received a sum of Rs. 60,000,000 as a loan from Khalid, for which the house would be held as collateral. It also said that Khalid had the right to confiscate the property should the loan not be paid back in a timely fashion.[18]

I was adamant when I told the SHO that I was party to the whole negotiation and that this agreement had been about leasing the property and not obtaining a loan from Khalid. I told him the

---

[18] Even though the lease was signed in Khalid's wife's name, husband and wife are looked as "one" in Pakistani culture, so technically any agreement done in the wife's name will automatically include the husband.

details stipulated in the lease and assured him that there was no discussion whatsoever of any type of loan. Furthermore, I pointed out to the SHO that the number of zeros had been altered in this agreement from Rs. 6,000,000 to Rs. 60,000,000.

My heart pounded faster and faster as I awaited the SHO's response. Everything was now in his hands. It was up to him to either let Khalid go or file an FIR, which would be law enforcement's way of saying that Khalid was indeed a suspect and, most importantly, that he would remain in lockup. If released that night, Khalid wouldn't just go back to his own life; he would leave his cell and head straight back to our house, invading our lives until a court decided otherwise. The house was already being occupied by his two female accomplices, one of whom, it turned out, was his wife—a Norwegian Citizen, in whose name this lease agreement had actually been made out and whose passport copy I had obtained earlier. The SHO was quiet and just kept staring at the agreement. I begged him with my eyes to see that it was a sham.

Then a light bulb went on in my head. Why not call Mr. Iqbal?

If a criminal's attorneys could aggressively aid in a crime, why couldn't I use my attorney as a shield against them. If my attorney showed up with his own law book and argued that the SHO was entitled to press charges against Khalid, maybe this SHO would feel a bit more confident in deciding whether this was a police matter or not. Surely everything Khalid had just done was punishable by law to the maximum extent. So, I sought the SHO's permission to call my attorney. He said he did not have any problem with that.

As soon as Mr. Iqbal was on the line, I explained the whole situation. Mr. Iqbal was very surprised to learn that Khalid turned out to be a crook. He said there was no provision in the law that allowed a person to seize and "occupy" a property by attacking the homeowner with guns, even if a loan agreement did exist. The loan holder would have to go through courts to legally repossess the property. Whether we could quickly prove that the agreement was a sham or not, what Khalid had done was illegal.

I asked Mr. Iqbal to come immediately to the police station and talk to the SHO about all this in person. I had this whole conversation right in front of the SHO, so he knew that I was being upfront and that I had not cooked anything up with my attorney to scheme my way out of this alleged loan agreement.

It was around 11:30 at night, however, Mr. Iqbal didn't want to come to the police station right away, so he asked me to hand over the phone to the SHO, and they talked for a few minutes. I could only hear one end of the conversation, but it appeared to me that Mr. Iqbal was doing a good job of convincing the SHO that this was all a scheme and that he had all the power in the world to not only detain Khalid but also successfully prosecute him. The SHO seemed to listen patiently and did not question anything. After the conversation was over, he handed my cell phone back to me. Mr. Iqbal was in my ear again, saying that he had made it clear to the SHO that this was a criminal matter and that he should deal with it accordingly. However, I still insisted that I wanted him at the police station.

Sadly, Mr. Iqbal outright refused to come. I told him that this was a huge ordeal, that my father was missing again, and that I needed his support. Mr. Iqbal still refused, saying he was a senior attorney and dealing with police directly in this manner was not his style (or maybe beneath him). I felt rejected but could do little else but hang up.

Luckily, this whole conversation had made an impact on the

SHO, even though at the time I did not realize it. He was a seasoned policeman, and I figured he must have some gut feel as to who was right and who was wrong. At least I prayed he did. I think he must have realized by this time that these scoundrels were victimizing us, but he remained undecided, and the time ticked by. I was becoming more desperate with every passing second. He sat in deep thought, just staring at the forged agreement. It seemed everything had come to a standstill, and my anxiety grew.

Another look at the clock told me it was midnight. That meant it was April 4th, the anniversary of my mother's death. She had passed away on April 4, 1999, in the very house Khalid was trying to occupy. Sometimes when I sit down and think about this in solitude, I wonder how much pain my mother's soul went through that night.

Soon after, the inspector came into the room and sat down with us. The inspector looked eagerly to his superior, awaiting further orders. It seemed to me he was silently asking the SHO, "Do you want me to let Khalid go or file an FIR against him and his accomplices?"

I had pleaded, I had begged, and I had a Supreme Court attorney confirm we were being victimized. I had made my pitch to the SHO, and I decided to remain silent, not even speaking to mention I was dead tired. The only thing I said was a silent prayer in my heart, deciding to leave everything to God. If being looted ruthlessly by these scoundrels were somehow written in our destiny, then so be it. But if it wasn't God's will, then we would get our house back. I had given this situation my last ounce and that was what was most important to me in order to satisfy my own conscience.

So, we all sat in total, consuming silence. The SHO could not seem to take his eyes off the contract and kept flipping back and forth between the three pages. Then he suddenly stopped, one page still pinched in his fingers, and looked at me. My heart was in my mouth. Every passing second dragged on for an hour.

The SHO gave the contract a final gaze and then slowly raised his head to address his senior inspector.

"Jao phar lo," he said, which means, "Go get 'em."

Those three words were perhaps the sweetest I have ever heard in my entire life!

Getting the home invaders

I jumped out of my chair in excitement. The SHO just kept his eyes on his inspector, barking orders that were music to my ears.

"File an FIR against this Khalid character and get him transported to central jail. I want it done tonight. Call the lady constable to arrange the immediate arrest of the two female intruders still inside that house."

The female constable soon showed up in the office to accompany us to the house. We reached the house around 12:30 a.m., and I was greeted by some police officers already at the scene and Ali on the front porch. Ali had, with police permission, put a padlock outside the door and locked the house so that no one could get inside or outside.

It's difficult to express the hatred I felt for these two criminal females as I walked through the front door.[19] Just looking at them, sitting there in the house I'd grown up in from age eleven, made me angry.

I told the police officers present at the scene that the SHO had

---

[19] I have a video of when I first entered the house and Ali and I had a conversation with these ladies. I will post it online if my attorney allows.

ordered the arrest of these women. I also asked police to search them both for any stolen items before they left the house. By that time, my brother's friend had also arrived with his three buddies, and my neighbor had also arrived with four guys of his own to help out. The women kept eyeing the gathering crowd, fidgeting nervously and looking as though they were pretty eager to get out of there. They became even more nervous when I searched their car with the help of police and found my sister's medical card hidden underneath one of the mats. It struck me then, as I held it in my hands, that had I not given my bag of important belongings like my US Passport to Aunty when I first landed in Islamabad, I might have lost them all to Khalid and his friends.

The two women tried to charm one of the officers, asking him if they could just get in their car and go home to get out of our hair. I reminded the senior officer that the SHO had ordered they be arrested and brought back to the police station. It didn't really help their case, either, when the police searched them and found our personal belongings crammed in their purses, such as some family photos, my father's business stamps, and letterheads from his bedroom. Even if they claimed they'd entered the house legally, they'd just been caught red-handed committing burglary.

With so many people present, things were becoming a bit chaotic around our house. Curious neighbors stood outside our gate, trying to peek over it, wondering what all the commotion was about. My brother's friend and three of his buddies were also helping out in any way they could, searching the two women's car and helping us keep track of them so they couldn't slip away. I did my best to gain control of the situation and made sure that the women were transported to the police station as soon as possible. The lady constable was, thankfully, all business, ushering the women out of the house, but she had to stop on the lawn because the police vehicle I'd seen earlier had been called back to the station for another case. Talk about living in a resource-starved country. In the end, it was decided that the two ladies would drive their own car back to the police station. I volunteered to follow them to make sure they didn't try to slip away.

Once we reached the police station, the women were brought to the SHO's office. I was moving to follow them when I saw my father sitting in a chair at the police station. He looked roughed up with his hair all messed up. He seemed pretty shaken by the ordeal but had his composure. I hugged him and greeted him in front of the SHO and told him everything was under control.

"When I got to the party, Khalid and his wife already had five guests I didn't know—four men and a woman. They asked why you hadn't come, so I told them, and then they asked me if I wanted to invite Peter over, so I did."

"They must have been trying to get all the men out of the house before they pulled their little stunt, the cowards," I said, realizing that I could have easily been held hostage that night, too.

"We'd hardly been there half an hour when they pulled out guns and put them to our heads," said my father. "Khalid said, 'Sit down and be quiet, or else.' Two of the men stayed behind to guard us, while Khalid and the rest of them went into our portion of the house. We sat there like that forever. I heard sirens, but no one ever came into the back portion of the house. The two guys didn't seem all that worried about the police, either, even when the commotion outside got pretty loud. About an hour later, one of the guys got a call. He sounded worried. He hung up and told the other one that Khalid had been taken into custody. They just ran and left us there. I called the police as soon as they were out the door."

I shook my head in disbelief at the sheer craziness of it all. "I'm so glad you're okay, Dad," I said, pulling him into a hug. "We'll talk more later. I want to be there when the SHO questions those two women."

I jogged down the hall into the SHO's office, where the SHO contemplated the two women across the desk. The SHO told them he was surprised by the brashness of their crimes. Khalid's wife acted as if she did not understand a word of Urdu. Later we learned that she, like Khalid, spoke it perfectly, but thanks to her initial ruse, the SHO only addressed her accomplice. She, however, just kept mumbling and did not give any straight answers. (During later court proceedings, we found out this woman routinely targeted wealthy businessmen in Islamabad with false rape allegations in attempts to extort money from them.) I recorded a video of this conversation for transparency. I will put it online after consultation with my attorney.

To my frustration, both of the women were let go that night, per the SHO's advice. He said that since police were still going to hold and prosecute Khalid, letting the women go would help to thwart any attack by their attorneys because it showed a mutual agreement to "something". We could fight the rest in court, but if we did not agree to something that night, the SHO feared that it would make it appear that he favored us over the other party. Only my father and I knew for certain that the agreement was forged; the SHO was just taking our word for it. He had to look neutral, and according to Pakistani law, if both parties come to some form of compromise or agreement, then the police are deemed to have acted in a neutral manner. My father agreed to the terms. Our "agreement" was that, if the women were let go, he would receive his house back in return. However, for the forgery charges, Khalid would be held and prosecuted. Nothing about it made sense to me, but given the circumstances, just agreeing with the SHO seemed like the best thing to do. I trusted he knew what he was talking about, and I wanted to help keep him out of trouble and on our side.[20]

The forged agreement was going to be difficult to dispute. It seemed as if some very neat photocopying and a good Photoshop job had been done on top of each other. The document looked super real and my father's signatures were somehow lifted from the original lease agreement. Overall, it looked like a valid sale agreement.

Profile of an international criminal

Khalid was kept in jail for only a couple of days before he was able to post bail. My father and I were not happy about it. Khalid and his wife were out free after committing forgery and armed burglary felonies.

Noor suggested we report Khalid and his accomplice wife to the Norwegian consulate. I also urged my father to do something about it. Finally, my father listened and took me and his secretary, Noor, with him to the Norwegian Embassy in Islamabad. He told the Norwegian authorities about Khalid and his wife—who both claimed to be Norwegian citizens—committing heinous crimes under the pretense of working for the Norwegian government. Naturally, the

---

[20] Khalid's attorneys later filed a complaint with higher police authorities against this SHO, claiming he favored Mr. Mubashar that night by expelling these women out of the house. However, the SHO's decision was found to be justified based on the uncovering of Khalid's extensive criminal background.

consulate staff members we spoke to were quite irked by this information. They asked for more details, which I was happy to provide. I gave them the copy of his wife's Norwegian passport and told them Khalid himself had refused to provide any ID. The Norwegian staff contacted the Kohsar police station SHO and asked him to provide complete details about the actions taken against Khalid and his wife, Naila Sharif. They said the matter was urgent, as Norwegian law enforcement, it turned out, was very familiar with Khalid.

The Norwegian Consulate delivered a fifty-two page report to Islamabad Police about Khalid's criminal activities in Norway, going back to the 1980s.

Khalid and his accomplices all belonged to an organized crime group called *Qabza* (English: Snatch). Their specialty is a relatively new form of crime in Pakistan that has become rather rampant in the last few years. Qabza groups develop and sign legal property agreements in one form or another with other parties. They then forge the contracts in their favor and snatch the properties from their rightful owners. As a matter of fact, while I was in Pakistan, two brothers who were casual acquaintances met with my father at his house to check on him and claimed that they had rented a house to some people who later converted the lease agreement into a forged purchase agreement. These poor brothers lived in England and had bought the property as investment, but now it had become a nightmare for them.

Police explained to me that this is the Qabza groups' favorite method of snatching property: creating a lease agreement in which they are a renter and then later claiming that they had purchased the property in full. The rent agreements allowed them to obtain signatures of the owners, making the forgery process a lot easier and more effective.

Below is a picture from the report that the Norwegian consulate provided outlining Khalid's extensive criminal history, including bank robbery and even murder. It turned out that, thanks to his crimes, he had been expelled from Norway and stripped of his citizenship.

WANTED: Khalid Mahmood.
Photo: Police

New social Security number
Norwegian police have hunted the Pakistani man for over two years. Shortly after he robbed the post office at Økern in July 2002, Mahmood was wanted via Interpol.

36-year-old needed Norwegian papers to get a new social security number in Sweden. With help from Norwegian tax authorities he established himself in the southern Swedish town of Lysekil and could freely operate from Sweden.

In the late 80s, Khalid Mahmood was convicted of the brutal Romsås killing.

A young Pakistani man was knocked down with the bat. Then Mahmood took his life through multiple stabbings. The penalty was ten years in prison.

Best practices
Mahmood was permanently expelled from Norway in 1995, and kicked out after completion of sentence. In 2001 he asked to get the entry ban lifted, but was rejected by the Directorate of Immigration (UDI). According UDI all information of the expulsion is available at the National Register.

The above is a copy of a small piece of the police report given to Islamabad Police by the Norwegian Consulate. (Date: April 2016, Source: Author).

Below is the letter provided by consulate staff to Pakistan authorities to counter Khalid's claims that he worked for the Norwegian government.

PTN Islamabad
Nordic police liaison office
Royal Norwegian Embassy
House nr 25, Street 19, F 6/2
Telnr.: 051-2077717

TO WHOM IT MAY CONCERN

Pakistani national Khalid Mahmood with Norwegian registration number 150169 26385 was deported from Norway in 1991 after serving his prison sentence.

Pakistani national Khalid Mahmood returned to Norway in 1998 using the alias Raja Wajahat Ali with Norwegian registration number 260972 19906.

He disappeared again in 2001.

Tove Aas Bechmann
Nordic Police Liaison Officer
Islamabad, 06 April, 2016

Actual letter provided to Pakistani police by the Norwegian Embassy regarding Khalid's criminal record (Date: April 2016, Source: Author)

As of this writing in early 2017, neither Khalid nor his wife has been prosecuted for their crimes. Khalid remains free on bail, and police cannot locate his wife. Maybe I will work with the Norwegian government to involve Interpol to get them arrested one day.

CHAPTER 24

BROKEN JUSTICE

The main reason I decided to write this book is to help my father get justice. The only way to do so is to make sure these culprits mentioned in this memoir are arrested and prosecuted. As I am finishing this book in early 2017, no one responsible for my father's harrowing ordeal has been apprehended. How can that be when police know their identities and have a good idea of their whereabouts? I won't go as far as suggesting that the police are colluding with these criminals, but the extent of aloofness and unconcern they have shown toward this incident is just mind boggling.

Pakistan claims to be a partner against terrorism alongside the United States, but how can a government which shows such complacency in catching everyday criminals ever expect to apprehend terrorists? It might be complacency, sheer incompetence, or a combination of both, but the fact of the matter is that dangerous criminals are loose in the country, and more must be done to bring them to justice. If nothing is done, their crime sprees will only continue, and innocent, mostly elderly civilians will pay the price.

In addition to reaching out to those in power in Pakistan multiple times, I have also contacted President Trump regarding this matter. My father's kidnapping is probably of little interest to the president, but I do have a larger question for him. If the United States calls Pakistan it's most important ally in the war against terrorism, shouldn't the president and his team want to understand the inner workings of Pakistani government and law enforcement?

If the President of the United States cares remotely about such issues, then I believe he should listen to this story and try to arrive at some conclusions about how to better engage with Pakistan. Pakistan promises the United States it will catch hardened terrorists in return for the billions of dollars' worth of aid it receives from the US, but Islamabad Police can't even catch identified kidnappers a few cities over? It's no wonder that after spending about a trillion dollars (yes, that's with a T) on wars in Pakistan and Afghanistan, the United Sates still had to take out its most hated enemy, Osama Bin Laden, itself.

Since my true tale gives an actual account of the inner workings of various governmental agencies within Pakistan, this book perhaps is a good read for various US government agencies such as the CIA, Pentagon, State Department etc., in order to really understand how the system actually works in Pakistan. If the United States ever wants to deal with Pakistan successfully, it must first understand how things actually work there. The United States' non-influence in South Asian countries stems from the fact that Americans typically do not seek to understand first before they want to be understood, and they are perceived to demand things from governments rather than working with them cooperatively. This creates a huge gap, and both parties fail to create a win-win situation. This is the core thesis of Stephen Covey's bestseller The 7 Habits of Highly Effective People, in which he encourages understanding the other party before making an attempt to be understood, whether you are a parent dealing with your teenaged child or an American President dealing with the leader of a Third World country.

Why did all this happen?

No matter how you look at this, all these happenings in Pakistan were coordinated attacks on my father to deprive him of his estate. Just how coordinated and interconnected is still up for speculation.

Even those who didn't have any direct involvement in these attacks still likely provided material and information to aid the kidnappers. That makes them accomplices. Riaz Khan's name comes to mind. Odd that his lawyer represented Khalid. It's also odd that Khalid attempted to do basically the same thing Abbas had done just a few months earlier—use false documents and violence to obtain my father's property. My father has achieved great success in life but has accumulated his share of enemies in the process. Seemingly, this group of enemies joined forces and carried out this assault on him in a highly coordinated fashion. Their attorneys were equally as guilty. Make no mistake; these attorneys are wolves in sheep's clothing. They are not merely legal counsel advising their clients. They also stood to benefit directly from any looting these scoundrels might have succeeded in. Khan's attorney reaped all the financial benefits of my father's hotel operations during the eight months Khan was serving his jail sentence. Then that same attorney just happens to be the same one Khalid and his wife call up after they invade another of my father's properties? Khan's attorney is not the only guilty party. Both Khan and Khalid had multiple corrupt attorneys working for them.

I am more than convinced that these attorneys struck some sort of deal to share in any monetary benefit that these criminals derived by looting my father. I had an attorney, too. If my highly respectable attorney refused to show up at the police station late on the night Khalid attacked our house, how did Khalid get not one, but three attorneys to eagerly run to his aid? Why were they so keen to help these criminals?

The connections between Riaz Khan, Ghulam Yasir Abbas, and Khalid Mahmood Raja run deep and are impossible to ignore. Police verified that Abbas used to stay frequently at Riaz Khan's hotel. Abbas had multiple FIR's registered against him by the police station that has jurisdiction over the hotel address. Khan's corrupt attorney was present at the police station the night Khalid invaded our house, once again trying to convince law enforcement that his new client's case was a civil issue, just as he had done with Khan's case.

It seems obvious to me that all these people must have known each other somehow. Khan and his attorney are both crooks with motive to get my father out of the way, and they had prior dealings with Abbas, who actually kidnapped my father. Khan's crooked attorney then represented Khalid, who also tried to take property from my father at gun point. For all we know, he or any of the three attorneys involved set Khalid loose on my father after they found out he belonged to a Qabza group, hoping that perhaps they could get some money out of my father's properties, as they had with the hotel. I'm convinced all these enemies are joined at the hip, and they all set their sights on my father's hard-earned wealth, determined to get it by any heinous means necessary. Abbas and his group even planned to stage a car accident and make it appear my father had died a natural death.

This targeting of white collar citizens happens all over the world, though the super-rich in developed countries like America are often slapped with frivolous lawsuits and bogus claims to try and extort money from them, rather than being kidnapped and brutally beaten, though that happens, too. Wealth always attracts the attention of malicious people. There are attorneys who specialize in finding ways to implicate the rich in frivolous lawsuits. This is not limited to rich people, but also large organizations. Companies are sued for the tiniest of things, things they can't control. These organizations are always working with their attorneys to devise strategies to put enough safeguards in place to thwart such lawsuits. In developing countries such as Pakistan, you are simply kidnapped and forced to part from your wealth via ransoms, forged documents, etc.

My father had accumulated enough wealth over his lifetime to attract the attention of the wrong kind of people, all ready to deprive him of his wealth. These criminals had a sound strategy, and I sincerely believe that it was God's hand that saved our family from this clever, evil plot.

When I questioned my father about how he could have erred so badly in not recognizing that something was wrong with Abbas and his business dealings, he was quick to point out that, by the same token, I had not recognized Khalid as a criminal even though I had met with him several times. I must admit he was right; I was not able to recognize Khalid as a crook. The only point I make in my defense is that he was introduced to me as someone already vetted by my father.

After all that's happened to our family, there is no point in blaming each other. The most important thing for my father now is to remain alert and avoid dealing with anyone with the remotest signs of shadiness in the future. We dealt with a number of exceptionally smart criminals. Although I had never met Abbas personally, I must admit, based on the two phone conversations I had with him, he sounded like a very nice guy. There was no way that by just a simple conversation with him I could have ever made out that he was a crook of such magnitude, though I had smelt something fishy.

To this day I have trouble believing we rubbed shoulders with an international criminal as dangerous as Khalid Mahmood Raja—a bank robber and a murderer. I not only met him face to face several times, but had even invited this killer inside our home when both my sister and nine-month-old nephew were present. Just thinking about this raises the hair at the back of my neck to this day.

I will not give up until all these criminals are punished for their crimes and my father gets justice. If this means trying to convince the President of the United States, or any other nation for that matter, so be it. Because these criminals are citizens of various countries, such as the UK and Norway, perhaps I will write to their Presidents one day.

As I finish this writing in February of 2017, one year after my father's kidnapping, Ghulam Yasir Abbas and his brother, Chaudhry Muqaddas Abbas (the man who sat in the back of the Toyota Vigo and told my father he was under arrest), are still at large. Sadaf Hassan Raza, who is purportedly a UK citizen, remains at large. Khalid Mahmood Raja and his wife, Naila Sharif, are still at large. So are their accomplices—we don't even know their identities. Riaz Khan, who has been illegally occupying my father's hotel since 2012, has served no more jail time than the eight months he received for his forgery charge, and he, too, is still at large. The hotel is locked up at the time of this writing.

Every single one of the criminals responsible for my father's year of hell are still on the loose, and so I continue to question where the justice in Pakistan is. Abbas and Raza are wanted suspects and are on the run. However, Khan and Khalid are both out on bail. They show up at their respective courts dates but still have not been sentenced.

So, I appeal to the President of the United States and other US authorities to instruct the Pakistani government to arrest all the criminals involved in this case. I appeal to the Pakistani authorities to provide justice to my father by making sure that these criminals are arrested and prosecuted. I appeal to the US border and international travel authorities to do better background checks on people who enter this country. It is my understanding that Abbas has entered the US multiple times in the past on a US Visa. Sadaf Hassan Raza has a free pass to enter the US if she is indeed a UK citizen. And finally, I appeal to the most important person: you, the reader of this book. If you believe you could help in any way imaginable, please don't hesitate to reach out to me. Also, your support via social media would increase awareness of this matter, so please follow me on Twitter and Facebook. You can easily find me using my full name, Syed Saeed Saqib.

I cannot not achieve my goal if you read this book and just put it aside. I am asking you to provide any assistance that you can, especially if you have the proper connections that can stir the pot and ask either US or Pakistani authorities to take swift action. As of this writing, I have contacted Pakistani authorities at various levels with very weak response or no response at all. Even the United States Consulate in Islamabad has not cooperated fully with my father, who holds a valid US Permanent Resident Card (otherwise known as a Green Card). In my understanding, the rationale behind it, according to immigration authorities anyway, is that a permanent resident staying outside the US for more than six months has abandoned his or her permanent resident status. But my father wants to come back here to the US and live with me and his grandchildren.

Bittersweet Homecoming

Despite my best efforts, I would leave Pakistan alone in June 2016.

Just as an extra precaution, my last few nights in Pakistan were spent in a hotel just behind PIMS. We had selected it because security was posted at the entrance at all times. Only Fiza and my father knew where I was staying. Ali perhaps knew, too, but he never said anything. With all of our enemies still on the loose, we feared word that I was leaving might result in a last ditch effort on Abbas', Khan's, or Khalid's parts to silence me. By then they must have known that I was Mubashar's son and that I had been a key force in helping him out of the messes they'd made and in protecting him from any plans they might have tried to put in place in regards to his properties. I did not kid myself that it was all over.

True, they were smart, but I had also given them a run for their money all these months, and they knew it. Their manipulation and torture had weakened my father, and without me to spearhead all the legal matters, things might have turned out differently. It could have taken days or weeks to get my father out of Shahpur. No one else had seemed willing to deal with all the police matters once we arrived in Islamabad, either. My father was sick, and Fiza and Ali had careers and everyday life to deal with. The Stay Order and biyan of 164—the only things that stood between Abbas and my father's properties— would not have been filed in time, and possibly would not have been filed at all. The biyan of 164 also pressured Raza into her confession. Abbas would never have been named or suspected. Even if the right documentation had been filed, my father would have been hard pressed to deal with the court dates, the three grueling days at the tax authority, the search for a magistrate, or any of the slow-moving legal processes. It was Ali and I who thwarted Khalid's meticulously articulated attack on my father's house through brutal force. Although I feel there was some divine intervention at work that night; I could have gone to the party and ended up being a hostage at gunpoint, too. Without me to counter not one, but three corrupt attorneys in the SHO's office, Khalid's phony document might have swayed the police; Mr. Iqbal certainly wouldn't have been of any help that night, as he had not even bothered to show up when I begged him and the SHO remained undecided to the last minute. I was certain our enemies were furious with me, and I wasn't about to give them an opportunity to get their hands around my neck.

I am someone who sincerely believes that when parents give you the gift of life, you also owe them something in return. All the struggles my parents endured to raise their children were flashing through my mind during all these months when I was helping my father out. I thought of my mother working hard at a new job right after giving birth just to buy expensive formula milk for me, and I thought of my father struggling and begging in front of General Zia-ul-Haq so that he could put a roof over his children's heads. While parents would never ask their children to return them any favors, I feel it is a child's duty to take care of his or her parents once they grow old and need help. And I would expect my son to do the same should, God forbid, such a horrible situation ever befall me.

I began saying my goodbyes two days before my flight was set to leave on June 4th. First, I took Peter and Noor out to lunch and bestowed each of them with a gift of cold hard cash to show my appreciation for all they had done for my dad. (Dolling out cash as a gift remains a common practice in Pakistan, while things like gift cards and pre-paid store cards are rarely seen.) Noor had played a key role in convincing my father to report Khalid to the Norwegian consulate. Peter had not only been at my side as we investigated the burglary damage and hunted down Khan, he'd also been held at gunpoint during the home invasion. He had been through a lot for us, and he'd never wavered. It was an emotional lunch. Noor cried when I handed her the gift, and both of them thanked me profusely for supporting them.

"Stay longer, Syed. Please," said Noor, still tearful.

"Yes, Syed, we still need your help," said Peter.

"I can't," I said sadly. "I *have* to go home. I have a life in the US. Two kids. They're waiting for their father to come home."

That quelled their pleas, but when we were saying our goodbyes, Noor insisted that she and I meet one more time before I left. That meant we'd have to meet the next day, and I was going to be busy. I asked her why it was so important, but she wouldn't tell me. I wanted to say I couldn't make it because I already had too much on my plate, but tears still shimmered on her eyelashes, and I just did not have the heart to say no to her.

When I arrived at my father's office the next day to meet her, she greeted me with a big smile at the front door.

"I'm going to have to make this short, Noor," I said. "I'm sorry."

"That's all right," she said. "Come inside."

Two big gift bags sat waiting for me on her desk. One was for my wife and the other was for my kids. I was overwhelmed with her generosity and thanked her for her kind gesture. We had all been through so much together. I was going to miss these people. The fact that my business in Pakistan was unfulfilled made it worse. My approaching flight filled me with a wide range of emotions that I struggled to make sense of.

On my last night in Pakistan, my father, Fiza, and I went out to eat dinner at a restaurant in Jinnah Supermarket. Between bites and some lighter conversation, we talked about all that had befallen us in the last few months and what would come next.

"The first thing I'm going to do when I get home is apply for your Green Card, Dad," I said.

He nodded and thanked me, but his smile was sad. We both knew it would take time.

"Fiza, you'll need to get a new passport and apply for a US Visa. I want you to come visit me soon."

"I promise I will."

After dinner, we dropped Dad at home. We got out to walk him inside, but he paused under the car porch, holding my gaze with an intensity that startled me.

"Dad, are you—?"

"Thank you, son," he said, his voice saturated with emotion. "Thank you for all you've done. I cannot ever thank you enough for how you've cared for me."

I hugged him and tears started to fall from his eyes. In the dim glow of the single light bulb hanging over the otherwise dark porch, I caught a glimpse of Fiza's teary eyes. Even as I hugged him, my father continued to thank me, over and over.

"Dad," I said, "there's no need. I've only done what any responsible son would."

I wished I could walk him, arm-in-arm into the house and stay with him that night, but I had to go to the hotel. Fiza dropped me off close to midnight, but the day's festivities and tears were still not over. Fiza pulled bags of gifts out of her trunk, laden with surprises for my wife and children. Beaming, I gave her a big hug and told her to drive safely home. I meticulously packed my things and then set my alarm for 4 a.m. in order to make my 9 a.m. flight the next morning before I finally collapsed into bed.

I woke up, bleary eyed, and took a shower, all the while praying that I would be able to hail a cab quickly. I had purposely not asked the hotel staff to arrange a cab for me. What if the criminals had discovered my hotel via cell phone tracking and bribed the hotel staff to have a cab waiting to kidnap me? There was no such thing as being too careful. But when I checked out into the morning air at 5 a.m., luggage trailing behind me and dangling from my shoulders, there were no cabs to be seen; it was too early. There were no toll free numbers in Pakistan – let alone a smart phone app – to hail a cab. You either go to a designated taxi stand or have to wait for one by the roadside. I waited patiently for a while, but I started to become nervous because the airline had advised me to be at the airport three hours in advance, meaning 6 a.m. I started walking briskly down toward the main road, looking anxiously back and forth across the lanes. At last, I saw one coming my way. I practically ran out in front of him in my frantic rush to get his attention. When I slipped inside, I asked him to stop by Fiza's house just two minutes away so that I could say goodbye to Ali. When I'd given him a hug and thanked him for all his help, Fiza and my nephew hopped into the cab with me, and we headed off to Dad's. He was already waiting outside the house.

"You're late," he said as he slipped into the front seat.

As he started giving the cabby unneeded directions, Fiza and I chuckled in the backseat while my nephew remained sound asleep in her lap.

The Islamabad airport was already hustling and bustling when we arrived, and the cab driver helped me put all my luggage onto the carts. Soon we were approaching the secure area, and it was time for the final goodbye. Fiza and my father turned dull, melancholy eyes on me. They looked almost lost, and I felt much the same way. What were we to do without each other? How would everything ever get resolved if we were apart? There was nothing to do but hug them both, hard and long. With quiet goodbyes, I turned away from them and started making my way to the secure area. As I approached the blind corner, I turned back for one last look and waved to them one more time. I have not seen them since.

My flight landed in Chicago in the afternoon. My wife and sons were supposed to be waiting outside. I yearned to get to them, but the long line at customs held me up for nearly an hour, and then the luggage conveyor awaited. I shifted from foot to foot as I watched the lazy turning of the conveyor, the slow trudge of colorful luggage. When I finally snatched the last of my bags, I dashed outside. There she was, at the exit door, my beautiful wife, my children at her side. I picked them all up in my arms one by one.

"Wow, you've lost weight," was the first thing out of my wife's mouth. I had lost thirty pounds in those four months.

We piled in the car, talking mostly of lighthearted things as we drove home, for which I was grateful. When I at last walked through my own front door, the sheer joy might have knocked me over, but underneath, I still felt a twinge of sadness. I looked beside me, where my father should have been. My son ran up and grabbed my hand. He eyed the many gift bags stuffed with colorful paper.

"What did you get for us, Dad? Can we open them, please?"

We sat in the living room and made an event of it. I pulled the gifts from the bags with flare, and my sons' faces lit up with each reveal. They bounced from one gift to the other, oohing and aahing. When my son took his Pokémon cards, I said, "I risked my life to get those for you. There were bad guys all around, but I knew you wanted them, so I made sure I got them."

That earned me the biggest smile of all and an innocent look of wonder.

When I tucked my children in that night, my elder son said, "Daddy, never leave us again for that long."

I hope I never have to.

www.ingramcontent.com/pod-product-compliance
Lightning Source LLC
Chambersburg PA
CBHW071158300426
44113CB00009B/1247